Money Making Vacation Rentals

Secrets to Market and Manage Your

Dream Home for Income

By

Beth Carson

Money Making Vacation Rentals

Introduction

This book is for anyone who wants to learn more about the world of possibilities with vacation rentals. Maybe you would like to explore the option of owning and renting out a future dream home. This book is for you. If you have just bought a new home and are interested in setting up your new rental using the Vacation Rental Industry's best practices, this book will guide you through the process. Experienced owners will also learn tips and hints to maximize sales and profits. For more information, please join us at www.VRFusion.com . Welcome to the wonderful world of Vacation Rentals.

A Caveat

What is shared inside these pages is real. Both the successes and the failures. But, of course, nothing can guarantee anyone's success, so please do your due diligence. Use this book as the guide that it is, and make thoughtful, careful decisions. Consult your accountant, your attorney, and your realtor, as well as local government, to make sure this is a good investment choice. There are no guarantees.

Acknowledgment

While I could have written this book on my own, I am so happy and grateful to the insight and additions that Sandra Cloer has made. She is strong where I am weak- particularly in pet friendly properties, organizing and training staff. I've learned so much from her through our decade of being friends and colleagues, especially in customer service. In fact, one year, I paid her way to come to Fiji with me and make my VR even better. That, and traveling with Sandra is a lot of fun. Adventure is around the next corner or at the next table. A true Southerner, she'll talk to anyone.

Even an expert knows when to call in help, and a new crew of bewildered but eager Fijian staff was definitely the time for my vacation rental in Fiji. Sandra not only taught them how to attack mold in the bathroom, she made them laugh and shared the recipe for ice cream soda- but with a Fijian twist- made with pineapple soda. They ask about her every time I come to Fiji, probably wondering why I don't have a pineapple ice cream soda up my sleeve.

Sandra is the driving force behind the raging success that is www.CranmoreCottages.com . She is a natural at 5 Star customer service, and has taken, "Smile when you answer the phone" to heart. She and her husband own 13 cottages and she manages 3 for others.

If you're in Hendersonville, NC, stay at Cranmore Cottages, mine at Elijah Gem Mine, and shop for antiques at Firefly, all owned and operated by the Cloers.

Chapter 1
Introduction to Vacation Rentals

Chapter Highlights

- Introduction
- Benefits of Vacation Rental Ownership
- Meet Your Consultants
- Benefits of Staying in a Vacation Rental
- Ways to get into the Industry
- Is Owning a Vacation Rental Right for You?
- A Few Perks of the Business
- Things to Consider

Vacation Rentals are the fusion of the best that travel and real estate have to offer. When you rent your second (or third or fourth) home out to travelers, you create an income stream that can pay your mortgage, utilities, advertising, and even provide a lucrative second income. You'll meet people from all over the world, either in person, e-mail or phone, and provide for an ever growing niche of travelers who desire more space and a better value than what hotels offer.

A recent PhoCusWright study has estimated the VR industry to be a $24.3 billion dollar market and growing. By renting your vacation home out to travelers, using the power of the Internet, you'll have low advertising costs with the potential for a high Return on Investment, or ROI.

Vacation rentals seem like a dream business. Who wouldn't want to own a piece of the most sought after travel destinations in the world and call it home for part of the year? Most of the time, it's a great business, but occasionally you'll have a difficult guest or crazy issue, like a flying squirrel landing on a guest while they are sleeping. (It happened to one VR owner!) Fortunately, these problems, flying squirrels and all, are rare, and it's a business that on most days brings joy to both owners and guests. All businesses have difficult areas, the question is making sure the business is a good fit for you. This is my passion and I'm thrilled to have discovered the freedom, both financial and lifestyle, that this business affords. I'm happy to share my success with you.

Benefits of Vacation Rental Ownership

Tax Deductions—Real estate offers significant tax deductions. In fact, my CPA owns several vacation rentals. Travel to your vacation rental is a legitimate tax expense if you are doing work while you are there. Mortgage expenses, utilities, supplies, furniture, and advertising are all deductible. Always check with your tax advisor, as tax laws change. Taxes are one area a DIY approach is not a good idea, unless you are qualified.

A Free Home—As with any rental property, the potential for having someone else pay your mortgage is a strong appeal. Imagine who much you'll make when the mortgage is paid off?

According to a recent study by G. William Dumhoff, of the wealthiest top 10 percent in America, 77 percent own real estate beyond their primary home. And while that includes many types of real estate, including commercial buildings, parking lots, and long-term rentals, none is as much fun to own than a vacation rental.

Income—Vacation rentals, in the right location and marketed well, can make significantly more money than a long-term rental. Unlike long-term rentals, you receive payment upfront, usually thirty days prior to their arrival. If they don't pay, they don't stay.

Growing Industry—the Vacation Rental industry is robust and healthy. Getting in now positions you in the market before others join the pack.

Meet Your Consultants

This is a journey to financial freedom and wealth, not a get rich quick scheme. It is a worthy business and the learning curve is manageable. Once you know the industry's best practices, you should have a higher income and a better experience for both yourself and your guests.

I fell into vacation rental ownership the hard way, after buying land and building a house with arrangements for the resort next door to manage and rent it. Whoops! The resort was sold during the construction of the home and the new owners needed to focus their attention on the resort and did not pick up the option to rent my home. I panicked, even putting the home on the market for a short time. Backed against a wall, my new husband recommended that I try to learn how to rent the property myself.

Hmm. There's an idea. After spending hours researching expensive print marketing opportunities, logging many hours on the computer, I stumbled onto the world of listing portals, and my success began.

While the resort had only promised 25 percent occupancy and would take over half of the income generated, using the techniques outlined in this book, I have been able to maintain an 85 percent occupancy rate while keeping all the profits. Visit www.starfishblue.com for more information on my dream vacation home turned rental in Fiji.

This was not my first foray into the wide world of real estate. I have rehabbed four houses and owns sixteen long-term rentals. Even though the long-term rentals are all profitable, put together, they make less annually thanmyone vacation rental in Fiji. I now consult for other VR owners, specializing in branding, marketing, writing, and web design.

Throughout the book, we'll hear from Sandra Cloer, owner of Cranmore Cottages in Hendersonville, NC. She and her husband, Dean, own 13 VR's and she manages 3 for others. She's a customer service guru and a great friend. We've traveled together to Europe, Africa, and the South Pacific, as well as the Carolinas and Florida, staying in vacation rentals. Together, we've learned from other VR owners- both their mistakes to avoid and their strengths to incorporate into our own businesses. This book is all the better for her contributions. You'll find her at www.CranmoreCottages.com

Benefits of Staying in a Vacation Rental

Do you know the vacation rental industry is as large as the cruise industry? One in ten North Americans have taken a cruise, and the same number has enjoyed the numerous benefits of a staying at a vacation rental. Worldwide, the numbers are likely higher. Vacation rentals have the highest customer satisfaction rate in the travel industry. They become more and more popular every year.

Why do people choose to spend their vacation in a home rather than a hotel or resort?

More space—Even with my small family of three, a hotel room is cramped. A vacation rental provides a bedroom for my husband to watch TV, a bedroom for my teenage daughter to Skype with friends, and a quiet living room for me to read at the end of a fun day of

4

sightseeing. Once you've stayed at a home with a well-equipped kitchen, separate bedrooms, and living area, you won't go back to hotels. Everyone is happy.

Privacy—Separate bedrooms are the norm at home, why not on holiday? Shouldn't your vacation be better than home, not full of uncomfortable comprises?

Economical—The facts bear out—vacation rentals are less expensive, on average, than hotels. Off-season opportunities are staggering. One family just stayed at a three bedroom, beachfront condo on Pensacola Beach, Florida for $150 a night. The grandparents stayed too, dropping the cost per family to $75 a night. Another family stayed at a three bedroom townhouse with a private pool in the backyard, as well as a community pool, four miles from Disney World for $75 a night.

Kitchen—having the ability to eat all or some of your meals in your VR saves money and gives you flexibility. Since meal portions at restaurants are frequently so big, many people eat lunch out and heat up the leftovers for dinner. This can save hundreds on each vacation. Breakfast at home is another easy way to save.

Amenities—VR's are the rock stars of the travel industry. While you can save money on fabulous finds, you can also get over the top amenities for a reasonable price. Three bedrooms, three bathrooms, in-room spa tub, private pool, private access to a beach with snorkel gear provided, an active reef complete with Nemo just steps from the house, and daily maid service. You can have it all at Starfish Blue, my rental in Fiji, starting at $250 a night. And, you get resort privileges at two nearby resorts for free.

Local Living—while it's true you can live like a movie star at a VR, you can also experience the rhythm of local life in a way a hotel does not allow. You can shop at local markets for regional fresh fruits and vegetables and interact with your neighbors, possibly developing life-long friendships.

Getting to know the owner and the inside scoop—You rarely interact with the owner of the hotel, let alone get the details on the best restaurants to visit and insider tips about tucked away spots the locals frequent. How about being told of free days at museums and galleries and off-peak times to visit local attractions? This is often the case with a vacation rental. Successful owners are friendly and engaging.

Ways to Get Into the Industry

There are a variety of ways people get into vacation rental ownership.

- Buy and rent out your retirement dream home
- Buy and rent out your vacation home
- Rent out an inherited home
- Convert a long-term rental to a VR
- Forced move requires renting out a home
- Business opportunity
- Retirement plan

Buy and rent out your retirement dream home - Do you know where you want to retire? Buying a home and renting it to travelers years before you are ready to retire is a great way to have part or your entire home paid for. It's a wonderful way to plant roots in a community as you will be returning again and again. You are an owner, not an outsider, and will have invested in your home and community. Compared with those that purchase at retirement, you will likely have paid far less for your home, and off-set a great deal of your purchase price by the income made from renting it as a VR home.

Buy and rent out your vacation home - Do you have a spot in the world that calls out to you in the middle of the night and during boring meetings? Do you long to spend much of your free time in one locale? If so, a vacation home can be a rewarding endeavor. I had been to over thirty countries before visiting Fiji. All of them wonderful, most worthy of a return.

While I liked Fiji, it wasn't until arriving at a resort at the very north of the main island that I found paradise. It was take-your-breath-away beautiful. The resort owner took some of the guests to the hill overlooking his dream—a residential area. I fell utterly and completely in love. The stars aligned, a choir burst forth into song--I had to have a spot there. And while it takes a mind-numbing twenty-four hours to get to paradise, it's worth every cramped second of travel misery. It's living a dream.

Your dream might be a bit closer to home. While it's possible to successfully manage a business from a world away, closer is better from a management standpoint. This is why Sandra Cloer, owner of Cranmore Cottages in Hendersonville, NC, started her business in her hometown, which is a tourist destination for other people. She is just a few minutes away from her guests, able to address concerns immediately.

Rent out an inherited home - The gift of a home when a loved one passes away is a treasure. Sometimes, it's hard to know what to do with it. If it's in a touristy area and in good condition, it could make a great vacation rental. And if the home is owned outright, making a profit is so much easier. Sometimes, multiple people inherit one home, so working out the details could get difficult. This is a case where a property management company could be a very good idea.

Convert a long-term rental to a VR - If you have a long-term rental that's right for the vacation rental market, this is a smart option, but generally requires more work than a set it and forget it long-term rental. As a landlord, you have a handyman in place or you do repairs yourself. You know the property well and generally don't have an emotional attachment to it. If your rental is in your home town, so much the better. A rule of thumb is that vacation rentals bring per week what a long-term rental will bring in per month. For example, if your condo rents for $1,000 a month as a long-term rental, it will likely bring in $1,000 per week. Look at your tourist season—- is it a place that will attract people year round, or does your area have a short season? Work that into your number crunching.

Making the switch from long term landlord to vacation rental owner is as much mental as it is physical. You'll need to furnish your home with thought and set up utilities, but instead of getting the occasional maintenance call, you'll be interacting with people planning a vacation. It's much more hands on, but more fun, if that suits your personality. If converting your rental to a vacation rental ends up not being a good move, you can switch it back to a long term rental easily, this time furnished, and command a higher price than an unfurnished rental.

Forced move requires renting out a home - If work or family obligations are calling you elsewhere, you may decide that keeping your home as a rental is a smart investment. Or, in a soft real estate market, it might be decided for you. Make sure you have the best mortgage in place before making the move, and remove all personal and sentimental items before renting it out.

Business opportunity

Some people get into the vacation rental business for the dollars and cents of it. Just as someone would open a coffee shop or a clothing store, they see VR ownership and management as a way to earn income. It's a worthy endeavor. Crunch the numbers.

Also, many property management companies earn commissions of 30%-50, so once you have success in marketing and managing your own property, managing VR's for other owners is a natural next step if you have time to devote to it. It can lead to full-time income.

Retirement plan- The US government allows for money in retirement accounts to be used to purchase real estate, under very specific rules, with a Self-Directed IRA. Instead of using stock and other financial products to grow your retirement account, you can purchase real estate. It's important to get advice from a qualified financial planner who knows the ins and outs of Self Directed IRA's, but this can be a way to enjoy your funds set aside for retirement and to leave a legacy for your heirs.

A Few Perks of the Business

Vacation, Vacation, Vacation. If your VR is nearby and you have an opening this weekend—why not go to the beach or mountains or wherever your VR is? Check with your accountant for current personal use restrictions on what the IRS deems a business, or you could end up cutting into your tax deductions.

Free Travel—trade unused weeks with other property owners for vacations all over the world. Most VR's will not achieve 100 percent occupancy. Turn some of those empty weeks into a free trip to the beach or the mountains. Paris, maybe? *Oh, la, la.*

Less Luggage—you can have an owner's locked closet for personal items that you don't want to share with your guests. Less packing means more time before, during, and after your vacation.

It IS a Small World—you have an opportunity to connect with travelers from all over the world. You are the expert for the locale, and people will look to you for advice. Travelers come to your town, and through your website, phone calls, and your Welcome Packet, you get to show off your favorite spot on the globe. And sometimes, when you've provided over the top service to appreciative guests, you might receive an invitation to their hometown.

Things to Consider

This is a hands-on business. To make the most money, you have to market and manage your property yourself. If you are already overworked, a property management company will likely be a good option for you, but be willing to pay for a good one. It will do you no good to sign with a poor company and save 5 percent on your commissions and miss out on business that a better management company could get you. To get the most reservations possible, consider having your own listings on listing portals, such as FlipKey, HomeAway, and VRBO, as you can handle the initial inquiries. No one will be better at selling the benefits of your property than you. Some people work out a hybrid situation, where they handle inquiries and sales, and the property management takes over when the guests arrive. Before choosing a management company, ask around to make certain you will be sure the level of service they provide both to your guests and to you as the owner are what you expect.

The occasional cranky guest. No matter what business you are in, you will deal with stressed, cranky people who aren't pleasant to be around. As long as you portray your home truthfully and deal with problems that pop up quickly most of your guests will be very happy. Occasionally, you will have a guest who is "unwinnable." No matter what you do, some people are determined to be unhappy. The good news is that with the highest satisfaction rate in the travel industry, these guests are few and far between.

People will be staying in your home. For some people, this reality is a struggle. Be honest with yourself and make sure you are comfortable with this, as people are paying you for use of your home. There needs to be a bit of detachment.

Homework

Where are you in the process of owning and managing a vacation rental? If you are considering it, look up your ideal locale on the internet. Look at real estate listings and vacation rental portal sites, such as FlipKey and HomeAway.

Why are you getting into vacation rental ownership?

_____

_____

_____

_____

_____

Have you ever stayed in a vacation rental? If so, what was your experience?

_____

_____

_____

_____

How would you do things differently as the owner?

_____

_____

_____

_____

If you haven't stayed in a vacation rental, try to book at least two short trips very soon. Look for places in the area you are interested in buying, and look for two different properties owned by two different owners. Write your experiences of **booking** here.

_____

_____

_____

_____

Write your experiences of **staying** here.

_____

_____

_____

_____

_____

Chapter 2
What Makes a Great VR

Chapter Highlights

- Buying Smart—Six Key Factors
- Buying the Property
- Inspections
- Insurance

Buying Smart- Six Key Factors

Before you dive in and purchase your own VR, there are several necessary features to ensure your success. Each of the six following factors should be carefully examined before you make your purchase.

Legally Allowed—This tip alone is worth the price of the book. An increasing problem in the industry is tighter restrictions, such as one month minimums and outright bans on vacation rentals. The hotel industry is feeling the competition and lobbying for tight restrictions or bans on vacation rentals. They are using scare tactics to stir up locals homeowners against the industry. It is urgent that you check with your local authority on any restrictions on short-term rentals. A simple phone call or two can save you the nightmare of starting a business that you cannot legally run.

While vehemently against the rights of homeowners being taken away, the fact is, they are. Do not buy in an area where your business will be illegal. If coffee shops were outlawed in your city, would you open a coffee shop? That would be madness. How will the authorities find out? The same way your customers will, through internet and other advertising. Once you purchase the property, it's critical to go through the proper steps to make sure that it is legally authorized as a vacation rental. Requirements vary widely, so check with your local government.

Location—anyone in real estate knows the importance of location, both the big picture—like beach, city, mountain; and the small picture—the exact location of the property in proximity to the major attraction of the area.

The most successful properties are located in highly touristic areas, like beaches, the mountains, or near major cities. Areas that aren't visited by many tourists but that do very well are near hospitals and universities. Is it in a safe area of town? Is it noisy? Does the home fit in the surroundings? Is the area already saturated with rentals? Is there room for yours?

Sandra: I was recently asked to manage a property. Three beds, two baths, walking distance to a lake. The possibilities were great. Until, that is, I saw it. While the house itself was gorgeous, it was the lone beautiful house in a dumpy area. The neighbors on all sides had tires piled up in the yard, cars on blocks, couches on the front porch. I could have taken pictures of just the house and the beautiful inside. I could have written it up to play up its positives, the proximity to the lake and downtown, the spacious living room, the tasteful décor. But I would have misrepresented a major aspect of the house. And in doing so, ruined someone's much anticipated vacation and my reputation. I had to decline the property.

Fact—not every property makes a good vacation rental.

Desirable—The property itself must be desirable. Your guests will first see your home on the internet, your curb appeal might be a balcony with a view of the ocean. If your place is very basic with no amenities, your only option is to decorate it well and adding a Wow Factor. Do not make it seem better than what it is, be ethical and truthful in advertising. Chances are, you'll have renters who are very glad for a budget accommodation.

Income—The financial burden of the property must be scrutinized before purchase. What are your goals for the property? Are you interested in supplementing your mortgage payment for your retirement home? Do you need to cover expenses on a house you can't sell? Do you want this to be a business and earn income from it? Spend time assessing your costs, including insurance, taxes, utilities, mortgage, and advertising. Costs also include time, either yours or payment for staff. Older properties generally cost more to maintain and upkeep than newer properties.

Amenities—What kinds of amenities can you offer your guests? Some will come with the home such as a pool, and some you can add, such as a hot tub, Wi-Fi, or flat panel TV. Different areas demand different standard amenities. We'll talk about that in depth in Chapter 5, "Wow Factor."

Safe—Visitors will expect that you've done any necessary work to ensure the house is structurally sound, free of mold and mildew, and safe electrically. Equally important, although harder to determine, is the safety of the neighborhood. Guests should be able to come and go without worry of theft or personal safety.

Buying the Property

If you don't already own a vacation rental, buy carefully. Choosing the right property can be the difference between a raging success and a deadweight. I want you to be a raging success!

Price

You've heard the saying, buy low, sell high. I advocate buy low, RENT high. Buying low is critical to the profitability of your new business venture,

15

as your mortgage will likely be your biggest expense. You control mortgage expense in two ways, the purchase price and your mortgage terms.

Technically speaking, market value is the price a person will pay for a house or condo. Listing price is often negotiable. If a house is listed for $300,000, but no one offers to pay that, then it is worth less. How much less? However much someone is willing to pay for it. Using a good Realtor should help you sort out both a fair price and potential rental income. They will then interpret the data, showing you how your prospective house lines up pricewise. There are many variables, such as square footage, view, condition, fixtures, and they will be able to suggest a price. However, it's up to you to determine what you are comfortable with paying.

It may take a while to find a property that is a good fit for you. In fact, Mike Sumney, author of *The Weekend Millionaire*, which focuses on long-term rental properties, says to expect to evaluate up to 100 properties before finding the combination of right property at a bargain price. Certainly, spending time looking through the newspaper, real estate flyers, recent sales, values based on property tax, and other market indicators is time well spent. That way, when you find a good deal, you'll know it.

Inspections

Always, always invest in full inspection. Would you spend a half a million dollars on a restaurant and not look in the kitchen, test the appliances, and make sure it meets city code for business? Don't walk blindly into this VR business venture. In some countries, inspections are unheard of. I would go so far as to say that it would be worth the time and money spent to fly in your inspector to look out for your best interest. Better to spend a few thousand upfront to find a major hidden problem than discover after purchase via the negative experience of a guest. Structural, electrical, or plumbing issues can cost you tens of thousands of dollars.

16

Ask your lawyer and accountant if putting your home in an LLC, or Limited Liability Corporation, is a good idea. Other options are available. Make sure you have a good umbrella policy. Get the most insurance you can. Getting insurance on vacation rentals is increasingly difficult, although not impossible. After the high level of damage in recent natural disasters in the past few years, and with so many vacation rentals being in coastal areas, insurance companies are fleeing risk, perceived or real.

Insurance companies are also concerned about vacancies. In a traditional home, a vacancy would mean a period of time where the homeowner/renter is living somewhere else, and no one is available to notice a leak or a fallen tree. So avoid using the word vacant. Put measures into place that will alleviate the insurance company's concerns of no occupancy, like having your cleaning person come every week, whether or not it is needs to be cleaned.

Now you have a tool box full of information to find a home you're happy with at the right price. After you make your purchase, it's time for the really fun part, making money!

Homework

Check to make sure short-term rentals are legally allowed both by your local government as well as your condo association or neighborhood homeowners association.

Contact

_____

Interview 3 Realtors, select one

Realtor _____

Realtor _____

Realtor _____

Contact 3 Insurance Agents and get quotes

_____

_____

_____

Chapter 3
Buy Low, Rent High

Chapter Summary

- Your Most Important Decision
- Break Even Comparison of Two Identical Condos
- Finding Great Deals in Real Estate
- Don't be Afraid to Look Outside the Box

Your Most Important Decision

The single most important decision you will make in your vacation rental business is the purchase of the property. This decision will affect your costs and your potential profit. It will also be a determining factor in how happy you are with your home. Look carefully.

Real Estate Fact: The price you pay for your home and the terms you negotiate with the bank will determine your income, both monthly and when you sell or rent. Carefully negotiating price and terms can save you tens of thousands of dollars over the life of the loan in what likely will be your largest bill—your mortgage.

Owning a vacation rental is not a get-rich quick scheme. But, with a little hard work, you can find a great property that will benefit your family and long range goals. The current downfall of the market does have an upside—homes are more affordable than ten years ago and interest rates, at the writing of this book in 2013, are at all-time lows, at least in the US. It is a buyer's market.

Plan on being in it for the long haul, both in the amount of time you look for a great deal on a vacation rental and the amount of time you plan to own it. This is a business. If you are interested in making a quick buck, this is not the right business. However, over time, you can be the proud owner of a home that many other people will have paid for.

Vacations are fun. You get to interact with people who are planning and living out dream vacations. It's easy to go into this business with blinders on. You have a near perfect experience on vacation, and it's very easy to project that into your money-making future. But choosing a vacation rental for your own personal stay is different from being the one responsible when the bills come in or when the phone call comes at 2 a.m. with a maintenance issue. It takes the right mix of a desirable property and demand for that property to be successful.

Break Even Comparison of Two Identical Condos

Buying low also allows you to profit when you sell, or rent, high. You can break even much faster than with a property that you paid a lower price for. You can't change the price you paid for a house once you've gone to closing. You can sometimes change financing through your bank, although it's not a guarantee.

Let's look at two nearly identical condos in the same complex.

20

Unit A Sold for $350,000		Unit B Sold For $220,000	
Monthly Expenses			
Mortgage	$3500	Mortgage	$2200
Condo Fees	$500	Condo Fees	$500
Electricity	$300	Electricity	$300
Water	$50	Water	$50
Marketing	$75	Marketing	$75
Total	$4425	Total	$3125

There are usually more expenses than this, but for simplicity we will just look at the most common ones.

If rented at a rate of $250/night, Unit A needs to rent eighteen nights a month to break even. Unit B needs to only rent twelve nights a month to break even.

Given the lower purchase price, the owner of Unit B could have additional monthly income which could be used on upgrades and amenities, which could possibly lead to a higher end product, and therefore charge a higher nightly rate and make even more money. Or, additional funds could go straight into the owner's pocket.

Buying low is half the battle in making your vacation rental a business success. However, it is not the only opportunity to do so. The following chapters are full of valuable information on marketing and managing your vacation home for maximum profit. Getting the most monthly income, by positioning your price just right—not too high, not too low, for utmost monthly income, is the second part of the equation.

High Monthly Income—Low Monthly Expenses= Profit

Finding Great Deals in Real Estate

When and if you sell your vacation rental, you should do so at the height of the season, when many happy vacationers are enjoying themselves and dreaming of the good life. So it makes sense, then, that if you are interested in buying at a discount, that you should do so in the off-season, when the vacationers have gone home, incomes drop, and people are willing to make a deal. If you buy in the off-season, understand that it may be a while before you see much income. Work the loss of income into your price point and make sure you have enough cash flow to get you through until peak season.

Where to look for an income producing vacation rental property

- Realtors: Start by sending out inquiries to qualified Realtors, letting them know of your interest, how much you are willing to spend and what you'd like to get for that amount of money. A Realtor who is a Resort & Second Home Property Specialist has taken a program offered by the National Association of Realtors. They will have specific training in this industry and can help point you in the right direction. Make a list of questions to ask them prior to your first meeting. This will help you both have a better understanding of what you are looking for in your new vacation home.

- REIA: Look at the local chapter of the National REIA organization (Real Estate Investment Association). Consider attending a monthly REIA meeting in the area you are interested to purchase in to familiarize yourself with the market and get acquainted with other investors. Becoming a member of a local REIA can offer up a world of insights—from the phone number of a trusted handyman to relationships with other investors. Sometimes, REIA investors will offer a property at a discount at a meeting in order to move their cash into a different project quickly. Membership costs are reasonable and are often a tax write-off. To find your local REIA chapter, visit www.nationalreia.com .

- Bank Owned Properties: There are two types of properties that banks deal with that will be offered at a discount. Foreclosures, where the homeowner is in default of the loan but still has a chance to make a payment that will save their home, and bank owned properties, which are properties that the bank now owns. Foreclosures can be tricky to get involved in. Often, you have to purchase the house without seeing the inside, as the homeowner still owns it until the sale, then often has a period of time to vacate after the sale. People can do a lot of harm when in a damaging life situation, and the inside could be a complete disaster. This also means forgoing a full home inspection, which is risky. As with the stock market, high risk can mean high rewards, but it can also mean losing a lot.

  On the other hand, a bank owned property has completed the foreclosure process and is usually represented by a realtor, giving you the opportunity to view the property and have proper inspections. The purchasing process is typically much slower with a bank owned property. But in the end, a few extra months spent getting a great deal can be well worth your time and effort. Check with different banks' websites to see what is available in the area you want to purchase.

- The Local Paper: you can subscribe to the local paper in the area that you are considering. You won't get it the same day, but having those real estate pages to mark up with circles is a fun part of the process. Purchase a large local street map in your target area and mark the prices of homes in neighborhoods you're interested in. You'll begin to see patterns emerge and when a deal is offered, you'll know it right away.

- Internet: There is a wealth of information to be had on the internet. Search for homes in the area you are considering, for example, Google "Homes for sale in Mayberry, NC" and your search should bring up local real estate listings, community information, and possibly travel and tourism.

- Surrounding Areas- When looking for properties, consider areas just outside a major city or tourist hotspot. Asheville is a major tourist destination- the number one small city in America for the arts. But Sandra's success comes from 20 minutes south of Asheville, in Hendersonville, NC. Hendersonville has a charming downtown with its own vibe, making it a destination in its own right, but it's certainly helped that in many search engines it comes up under "Asheville Area."

While "Bedroom Towns," or towns that are within commuting distance from a major attraction, are an option, they often don't have anything of their own to offer except homes and grocery stores. It is best if the town you choose has something of its own to offer. For example, Alexandria, Virginia, is near Washington D.C., but is a destination in its own right. Old Town, the waterfront, the Torpedo Factory, and scores of blocks of quaint shops, restaurants, and homes give travelers to Washington D.C. who stay in Alexandria a choice—go sightseeing in the nations' capital or explore their temporary home base.

Don't be Afraid to Look Outside the Box

- International: often, the best deals are to be had beyond well-traveled locations. For example, if you are looking for a perfect diving spot, look for properties in Belize instead of in the Florida Keys. Not only are they more affordable, there is generally less competition, and as it's closer to the equator, a longer season. The more adventurous you are, the further afield you can look.
- Look for your interest, then find it somewhere less visited. While New York has it all for a big city, prices are enormous for a tiny piece of apartment, usually with compromises, such as miniscule bathrooms, micro-kitchens, and 4th floor walk ups.

Atlanta offers similar amenities of theater, museums, galleries, and shopping at bargain basement prices. Buenos Aires also has world-class culture, beautiful art galleries, and European architecture, for a fraction of the price. Any experience you want out of a vacation rental (beach, diving, culture, art galleries, snow skiing, mountains), can be found at an attainable price.

For the very adventurous, seek out the latest trends in travel with travel magazines. Costa Rica was Nirvana for travelers and buyers alike for a number of years. This country with coastline on both the Atlantic and Pacific Oceans is close to the U.S., safe, offers a wide range of eco-tourism options, and, for a while at least, low home prices. Soon, the market was saturated with buyers, and prices went up. Travelers started to notice Panama, and the same thing happened there. Bargain hunters are now searching Nicaragua. In five or ten years time, another country will top the list. Backpackers are usually the first to discover a place with potential. World travelers follow, and as their demand grows, infrastructure is built around it, and opportunities for VR investors are best at this time, before the boom. Those who bought early can benefit from the ongoing visitors, because they paid a much lower price. Those entering the market during a seller's market, when real estate supply is low, will have a harder time making a profit from their vacation rental.

A location close to the equator can provide a fifty-two week season. Are there enough travelers to get fifty-two reservations? If the market is saturated, it will be hard. But if it's off the beaten path, there could likely be enough business to support the idea. Read travel magazines and see if you can spot the next travel trends. See Chapter 4 for more details on the international market.

- Lipstick Deals: A "lipstick deal," is a property that only needs cosmetic fixes like carpet, paint, and maybe new countertops. It is also a viable option for the investor that wants to get a great price without too many headaches. If you lack fundamental carpentry, plumbing, and electrical skills, a full redo will be very expensive and complicated, with issues involving code, plumbing, electrical, and structural. If you are handy and have past experience, a fixer-upper is a great way to get into the market at a lower price point. However, always weigh the time it will take you to do everything yourself.

- Fractional Ownership: some people confuse this with timeshares. I do not recommend time shares as a way to get into vacation rental ownership. Fractional ownership, however, is an avenue worth exploring if you do not have the money to purchase a property independently. The property is divided by time, between two to twelve people, and each person gets access to their time based on the amount of investment. An important variable is what time slot you will receive. Time slots can be divided any number of ways, including monthly and on a rotational basis. Another variable is how the property will be managed. What if you have differing opinions with your co-investors, like décor or landscaping? Do your research well before entering into a fractional ownership.

Homework

Look at prices for homes in your target area then determine what price you are willing to pay. Check your credit score, then determine your interest rate; banks will often give you a quote over the phone.

Using an online mortgage calculator, determine what your mortgage will be. Adjust up in case there is an interest rate hike between now and the time you purchase.

Mortgage	$_____
Taxes	$_____
Insurance	$_____
Marketing	$_____
Homeowners' Association Fees	$_____
Utilities	$_____
Repairs	$_____
Maintenance and housekeeping	$_____
Travel	$_____
_____	$_____
_____	$_____
_____	$_____
_____	$_____
Total	$_____

How many nights a month will you need to rent it to break even? See Chapter 7 "Evaluating Your Position in the Market" for more information.

Finding good deals in real estate—the price you pay affects your bottom line, month after month. Do the necessary work now to get the best deal.

Realtors: look for Realtors with the Resort and Second Property Specialist Certification.

List three Realtors in your target area

_____

_____

_____

REIA's: Join your local REIA—Real Estate Investor's Association.

Bank Owned Properties—Look at websites for homes that have already been foreclosed on.

Check three bank websites in your target area.

27

_____

_____

_____

The local paper—have the local Sunday paper delivered to your home
and start learning about different neighborhoods and trends.
The Internet—you'll see lots of photos and some virtual tours.
Make notes about the top five listings you see.

    1. MLS # _____

_____

_____

_____

    2. MLS # _____

_____

_____

_____

    3. MLS # _____

_____

_____

_____

Surrounding Areas- consider going slightly outside of your target area
for huge savings, but realize that your rental income will be affected by
this.
List 3 other areas that have solid potential

    1. _____
    2. _____
    3. _____

International—Are you open to the international market?

_____

If yes, where?

    1. _____
    2. _____

3. _____

Fractional Ownership- look carefully at this alternative to buying outright. If you are interested, do a lot of research on the risks, pros and cons.

Chapter 4
International Market

Chapter Summary

- Introduction to the International Market
- Benefits of Buying Overseas
- Risks vs. Rewards
- A Few Perks of the Business- International Style

Introduction to the International Market

Vacation Rentals are an international phenomenon. Nearly every first or second world country has them, and even a few third world countries. The world is truly your oyster. As airfare gets more competitive and flying times shorter, the world is getting smaller. Don't rule out a vacation rental near skiing in the Southern Alps in New Zealand, a home near fly fishing in Chile or a tropical getaway in Belize. These can be economic alternatives to the similar experiences at home.

When considering an international vacation rental, consider the additional commitment required. New country, new policies, additional travel. The purchasing process can be more difficult than buying a home in your country of residence. In fact, Sandra's business model of purchasing in her home town, has paid off fabulously. Of course, she's always in the midst of her work and she needs to actually go on vacation to get a break. But it's practical. Pragmatic.

There's nothing practical about buying a piece of property in Fiji. This is exactly why it worked for me. I follow my passions and love a challenge. But make no mistake, the complications are more difficult to address from a world away.

Benefits of Buying Overseas

Competition can be scarcer in other countries. HomeAway currently lists thirty-four vacation rentals in Fiji. FlipKey has twenty seven. In Hendersonville, NC, where Sandra owns her properties, there are more VR's than the entire country of Fiji. Fiji has plenty of visitors looking for a vacation rental experience. This provides a high occupancy in my South Pacific home.

Travelers who stay in vacation rentals travel more often and are more likely to travel internationally. They also spend more money than the average traveler, according to PhoCusWright. Purchasing a vacation rental abroad is somewhat of a calculated risk, as we know vacation rental travelers are looking abroad for their holidays and VR homes to stay in.

Property—beachfront, ocean view, mountain, etc., can often be had for a small fraction of the price you will find it listed for in the U.S., Canada, or parts of Europe. In fact, land can be cheap, dirt cheap. Beware of building costs and time involved in construction. The costs can be more than budgeted and length of time to build can be significantly longer due to fewer resources and different standards.

In fact, when I was building Starfish Blue, I used a builder that was recommended for the quality of his work but had a reputation for being late on the job. He promised the house would be built in sixteen weeks. "I'm staking my reputation on this. I have to redeem myself." Three years later, after serious intervention and phone calls, faxes, threats, cajoling, and tears, the house was ready for guests. The moral of the story? Land is cheap, but costly if it takes years until you have income. Look at existing homes, where you can inspect the quality of the work and have a place up and running in no time.

Your profit margin has the potential to be much higher in foreign countries, as you are dealing with local real estate, which can cost less, yet renting to foreign travelers, who expect to pay more. Your guests, for the most part, will come from North America, Europe, and Australia and NZ, where incomes allow for a luxury vacation. If you purchase in an up and coming market, somewhere a bit more off the beaten path than say, Paris, you should see a huge difference between income and expenses.

Risks vs. Rewards

Foreign investment isn't for everyone. You have to find a place you love, love, love, buy or build a home there, and then somehow, it turns into a place where you work.

As with the stock market or any other investment tool, the highest rewards carry the highest risks. For example, a startup company that you can get for $1/share can skyrocket, doubling, tripling, and more overnight, but it can also tank overnight, leaving you high and dry.

There are endless unfamiliar practices and customs—this isn't Kansas. It truly isn't. I love Fiji, but it can be daunting to accomplish tasks that we would find commonplace in a Western country.

In Fiji, just getting electricity required forms, a photograph each for myself and my husband, our thumb prints, and a visit to the justice of the peace. In the U.S., it can be handled with a phone call. To get Fiji's version of pension for my workers, involved a similar amount of hassle, plus a police report from my hometown. I had to go to my county jail (a place I had never been before) to get my clean rap sheet. Wherever you invest, check into regulations and requirements.

Depending on the locale, local politics can be tricky to navigate. Bribes are not uncommon in many areas, and some areas are distrustful of outsiders. Spend some time at your dream locale to see if you can find any potential trouble spots. Talk with other foreign property owners to see if they can forewarn you of any potential roadblocks and how you can avoid them. Ask other owners if they could have a do-over, if they would reinvest in the area.

Each country has their own particular process for doing things. Their systems must be followed, no matter how crude or over laden with paperwork you think they are. Remember, you are in their country. The more you know before you invest, the better off you will be.

Here are some surprising norms I have discovered when looking into investing abroad.

- In France, you have to pass a medical exam to get a mortgage.
- In Argentina, real estate transactions are handled in cash.
- Mexico—while its laws are in constant flux, real estate currently needs to be purchased in a Trust with at least one Mexican. Your lawyer will often fill the role.

Securing a loan abroad can be difficult. Many vacation rental owners who invest overseas use equity in a current home to purchase the overseas home outright. That is a risk to be carefully considered.

A Few Perks of the Business- International Style

Become member of community—you'll be part of a community in a way that you could never be as a visitor. You will furnish and supply your house from local merchants, decorate with regional artists work, use local utilities, and employ members of the community.

Diversify—It's always a good idea to diversity your real estate investments. If you have a low risk, reasonable reward property, you have the opportunity to balance it with a high risk, knock your socks off good reward property. Buying internationally makes even more sense if this is your second VR. Consider alternating peak seasons like homes in different regions tropical and mountain.

Long rental seasons—the closer you get to the equator or if you buy in a timeless city like Paris, you will find you are booking guests throughout the year. My Fiji property gets North American and European visitors as well as Australians and New Zealanders, providing a year-round season of people in opposite hemispheres who are eager to escape their winter.

Specific Marketing—people the world over look to the internet for planning their next holiday or vacation. While FlipKey and HomeAway and the other industry powerhouses make sense, look at the smaller listing portals that focus on your area, as well. Travelmaxia has an amazing business model and focuses only on the South Pacific. Do a search for your locale and either "vacation rental," "holiday home" and other variations, like holiday lets, vacation condos, baches (a small New Zealand beach cottage) or whatever else suits your home.

You have to do your homework when investing overseas. I recommend using a realtor who specializes in dealing with foreign buyers. They will anticipate what will seem atypical to you. Usually, foreign investors are eager to talk to someone else in the journey, so contact other foreign owners in the area and ask for recommendations. Most people will be very happy to talk to you.

Potential of emerging market—Ecuador has the potential to be next Costa Rica at a fraction of the price.

Note that while things can be more difficult in another country, your guests often expect that. One of our guests in Fiji even brought their own headlamps for evening walks to the resort (we provide flashlights.)

Thoughts from someone who's been there, done that, and lived to tell about it.

It's easy to bring your own experiences and expectations to the home buying process. The Western way of doing things is pragmatic and quick. Time is of the essence. Relationships are for your friends and family—for after you come home from work.

In most other countries, it's the opposite. Before business is even spoken about, relationships are formed, cemented over tea or a long afternoon lunch. Possibly many of these such meetings. Only then can the possibility of a working relationship begin.

Things take time. A lot of time. Sometimes, a bewildering amount of time. From establishing trust in the community to building a house to painting a room, the rest of the world doesn't move at the pace that America and the rest of the industrialized world does.

And that's a very, very good thing. We go to places to escape what we have created. We need to not bring the same issues with us.

Homework

What experience are you looking for? Relaxing on a hammock on a deserted beach with fabulous view? Swishing down the mountains and a lodge home to come home to? Big city options with history?

_____

_____

_____

If you've traveled internationally, what is your favorite place?

_____

_____

_____

Why? List as many reasons as possible.

_____

_____

_____

_____

_____

_____

_____

Find out as many of the negatives about purchasing a home in your desired locale. Just as you would spend some time dating someone before marrying them, hopefully discovering as many of their flaws as you could, see if these are negatives you can live with.

Negatives

_____

_____

_____

_____

_____

What are the tax laws in your country of choice?

_____

_____

_____

_____

_____

Restrictions?

_____

_____

_____

_____

_____

If you are still interested in purchasing overseas, celebrate, and welcome to the club of overseas owners!

Chapter 5
Wow Factor- Step Ahead of the Competition

Chapter Summary

- "Wow Factor"
- Inspiration
- Low Cost "It Factors"
- High End Wow Factors

Have you ever stayed in a resort or hotel that had a wow factor? Something beyond the expected. Maybe it was a five story, open air lobby with a view of white sand and blue water. Maybe it was a cold glass of fresh juice served to you while the bellman took your luggage to your room. Maybe it was a foot massage upon arrival. It instantly brought you out of hectic travel mode and into vacation mode.

Wow Factor

The most successful vacation rentals have it. And unless you are building a home, you can't create "Wow" so easily in the structure of your vacation rental. But you can create a memorable, over the top, beyond expectations experience that your guests will say *Wow* about. Your best marketing comes from people that have experienced your holiday home and come home bragging about their experience, either to their friends at the office or soccer field, or a million strangers on TripAdvisor.

People are looking for an experience when they are on vacation. They are choosing a home over a hotel, something only about 10 percent of the population has done. This is your chance to shine, be it something as simple as a hammock in the yard, rose petals on the bed, or a high end in-home theater. You have the opportunity to give them a vacation they will never forget.

Location, Location, Location

Some homes intrinsically have the wow factor based on location—like being absolute beachfront or on a mountain ridge, or a penthouse view of the city skyline. Your home doesn't have that? Not to worry, you can create it.

First, check out the competition. Take an hour and look at the listings in your area. If you have a condo, look at condos, if you have a house, look at houses. What's expected for the area? If 90 percent of the homes have wireless included, that's a standard amenity, not a wow factor. But, if you have a cabin in the middle of nowhere, and no one else has Wi-Fi, that could be considered a definite upgrade to their experience.

Inspiration

Browse through some travel magazine articles. What accommodations have really captured your imagination? The vacation rental in Jamaica that came with its own chef. The holiday home on a tiny island—the only house on the small patch of land. A tree house for the kids. Snow skiing out the front door. Magazine articles need more than the kitchen and one and a half baths. They seek out the extraordinary. To really stand out and have people lining up to stay at your place, you need a wow factor.

What's important to you when you travel? What would be travel magazine article worthy? Dream a little, then make a list of five possibilities of what is feasible to do in your VR.

1. _____
2. _____
3. _____
4. _____
5. _____

Now, spend some time looking at the competition. List the top ten features that stand out from the crowd. Then, list the number of times you see it. Keep an eye out for your ideas as well as new ones.

1. _____
2. _____
3. _____
4. _____
5. _____
6. _____
7. _____
8. _____
9. _____
10. _____

Be sure the properties are meeting the norm for amenities in your area. Are hot tubs standard? Better make sure you have one, too. Look closely at what's there and what's missing. Is the décor bland and tired?

I ignore vacation rentals that have drab white walls and tired furniture. After looking through many vacation rentals on Pensacola Beach, Florida, I found a gem of a property with red walls, art, and stylish but not overwhelming design.

When the owner wrote back immediately with a quote and answers to questions, I booked on the spot, delighted with the place. Red walls cost no more to paint than white walls, and while the furniture had been chosen with an eye for flair, it was not expensive furniture. But it was enough to make the reservation.

Low Cost "It Factors"

Hammocks: this is an easy one that pretty much anyone with a porch, deck, or yard can do. If you are tight on space, you can take one end of the hammock down, and hang both sides from one side of the porch. The guests can hook the other end when they want to use it. Or, get a hammock chair.

Large selection of DVD's, CD's, and Books: some people go on vacation to just have a chance to hang out. They may work crazy hours or live the typical Western lifestyle of too many activities and not enough time. The ability to relax and unwind may be just what they are looking for. Target and Wal-Mart generally have a selection of $5 videos, and used book stores are great for finding a variety of books that will suit many interests.

Guest Amenity Packages: this is an amenity that the guest pays for—making it a perfect situation for you. But the fact that you've arranged it for them will make your VR stand out from the crowd. Have a small selection of upgraded amenities—like wine and cheese, chocolate covered strawberries, sparkling champagne (with a non-alcoholic version available) an in-home masseuse visit-- the sky's the limit. You can also do the same for birthdays—have a cake and balloons, a Girls'

Weekend with feather boas and chocolate; what appeals to your clientele? As the guests are paying for these, it's the option to have it arranged that appeals to the guests. It's bridging that gap between a hotel experience and a guest experience.

Sound System: I recently added an indoor/outdoor sound system to Starfish Blue in Fiji. Now, it's not just a pool, with a stunning view of islands, it's a pool with your favorite music. A simple cable from the electronics store and easy directions let anyone with an iPod or mp3 player can bring their own music. Some people even make up their own mix, and every time they hear the music, they mentally fly back to Fiji and Starfish Blue.

Game Room: do you have a basement or other room that is clean and serviceable, but doesn't really serve a purpose? Add a pool table and other games, and you have an immediate draw. In fact, in some areas, like the Outer Banks of North Carolina and Gatlinburg, TN, they aren't unique, they are standard issue in larger houses.

Flat Panel TV: this is an easy upgrade. For around $500 you can give wow factor to a budget property. Flat panel TVs are standard in higher end properties, and becoming more common in lower end properties.

Décor: you can slap some paint on the walls and throw some furniture around the perimeter of the room, or you can select paint colors and décor thoughtfully. You can use a designer, but often a few hours spent flipping through magazines for inspiration for eye catching design will give you enough inspiration to work with. Shop at high end bargain stores and in the clearance section for inexpensive items with high visual appeal.

High End Wow Factors

Location, location, location! If you have an oceanfront home, or a penthouse condo with a stellar view of the city skyline, you already have your wow factor. Feel free to upstage the competition by adding more.

Private Pool: if you have space, this amenity will add bookings for people who want to spend more time relaxing, and less time traipsing back and forth to the beach. Be sure to factor in upkeep into your budget.

Hot Tubs: in some areas, these are standard. If not, this is your wow factor.

Daily Maid Service: this is feasible if you have a high end property with the rates to off-set the cost, or have an international destination where wages are low. In addition to decreasing the hotel/home gap, this provides local jobs. This can also tip the scales in your favor for guests who are undecided between a VR and a hotel.

Private Chef: High end guests don't want to cook every day, but they might not want to eat every meal out. A private chef would be a decadent treat for some, and for wealthy clients, might be part of their everyday life that would be hard to give up during vacation.

Hanging Bed: At Starfish Blue, I designed and added a covered, hanging bed with a view of the ocean and 3 islands. Some people even spend the night on the bed. What an amazing vacation memory.

Media Room: If you have an interior room or one you can put black out curtains on, it might be just the place to put a media room. You'll need to invest in surround sound, a projector, comfortable seating (consider building risers so everyone has a great view) and even a popcorn machine. Watch your bookings go up.

Ideas: look for ideas in Realtors' Open Houses, home and travel magazines, and television shows on the Travel Channel and HGTV, to name a few. As vacation rentals are a blend of hotel and home, don't rule out hotels as a source of inspiration. Hotels are noticing the trend towards more spacious, private accommodations, and we should respond with what they do right.

Homework

After doing the above research on your competition and in magazines and hotels, make a plan to implement three wow factors in your vacation rental.

1. _____

   Steps to make it happen

   _____

   _____

   _____

   _____

2. _____

   Steps to make it happen

   _____

   _____

   _____

   _____

3. _____

   Steps to make it happen

   _____

   _____

   _____

   _____

Chapter 6
Evaluating Your Position in the Market

Chapter Summary

- Comparing Your Home to the Competition
- Worksheet —Comparing Your Home with Three Like Properties
- Comparing Occupancy
- Looking at the Competition in Your Price Range
- Setting the Price

Well done! You've chosen a home that is high on the list from Chapter 2, and have found a house where it is legally allowed to rent on a short-term basis, has a great location, is a desirable property, the numbers work to provide income, it has amenities that people are looking for, and is in a safe area. Now, we need to see how your home compares to the competition in your area. Let's evaluate it.

Comparing Your Home to the Competition

The first step is to make a list of your home's features. Using the form below, take some time to look at everything your home has to offer. If you don't have a second home yet, use the form to be realistic about what you might actually purchase. Put yourself in your guests' place for a few moment, and realize that they will not see your home by itself. They will be comparing it with numerous other properties. You need to do the same.

Comparing Your Home with Three Like Properties

As you can see, we'll be asking you to look carefully at three other properties. Do a search for the town your vacation rental is in, and take a look at the listings. Do a Google search as well as look at HomeAway, FlipKey, and VRBO.

Look only at homes that match your criteria in your immediate area. If you have a studio, don't look at three bedroom places, and if you have a home five miles from the beach, don't look at oceanfront properties. Get as close to your property as you can.

Look closely at the three most appealing. Really look at their listings. What do you notice? Jot down some notes here as to what grabs you as a potential renter—good and bad.

Fill in the worksheet for the three comparable homes. Use the blank lines for amenities that are important in your region. For features that are subjective, such as location desirability and kitchen, use the grading scale of A-F, "A" being the best, and "F" being lacking.

Worksheet

VR Comparison Worksheet	Your VR	A	B	C
Number of Bedrooms				
Number of Full Bathrooms				
Number of 1/2 Bathrooms				
Square Footage				
Number of similar VR's				
Number of Guests				
Game Room				
Hot Tub Private				
Hot Tub Shared				
Pool Private				
Pool Shared				
Fire Place				
Cable or Satellite TV				
Flat Panel TV				
TVs in all bedrooms				
High Speed Internet				
Parking				
Washer/Dryer in Home				
Washer/Dryer on Premises				
Walking to attractions				
Dedicated parking				
Local Attractions Grade A-F				
Location Grade A-F				
Kitchen Grade A-F				
Condition of home A-F				
Amenities Grade A-F				
Neighborhood Grade A-F				

Comparing Occupancy

For occupancy, look at the three properties' availability calendars. Calculate the occupancy for the next three months. Just take the total number of days, around ninety, and let's say forty-five are filled; that's a 50 percent occupancy. Excellent in the off-season, not as great in peak season. Some markets fill quickly, others have many last minute bookings that will increase these numbers. Also note that many owners do not take time to keep their online calendars current, or use it at all. Keep this in mind if you find a comparable property with no bookings. This is a way for you to stand out from the crowd and be taken seriously. To be safe, look at ten calendars in your area. Take note of the last time they were updated.

Comparable 1

_____

_____

_____

_____

_____

_____

_____

Price per night low season $_____

Price per night high season $_____

Price per week low season $_____

Price per week high season $_____

Occupancy _____

Comparable 2

_____

_____

_____

_____

_____

Price per night low season $_____
Price per night high season $_____
Price per week low season $_____
Price per week high season $_____
Occupancy _____
Comparable 3

_____

_____

_____

_____

_____

_____

_____

Price per night low season $_____
Price per night high season $_____
Price per week low season $_____
Price per week high season $_____
Occupancy _____

Looking at the Competition in Your Price Range

Now, use this information to determine how comparable your property is when evaluated against your competition. This is not a science, you're going to have to use old fashioned common sense. If you have an identical house, but your house has upgrades, such as a game room in the basement where your competition has nothing, you can charge more. The same is true if your house is below the standard for your area- some renters are willing to overlook tired décor and older appliances for a bargain price.

Setting the Price

Now you can determine a fair price for your rental. You may want to repeat the comparable search with a few more VR's before determining a price, but you should have a good idea at this point. You should be able to at least set a range, per night, and per week.

As a new property, don't make the mistake of setting your prices too low or too high. Instead of setting your prices too low, add an incentive or discount. People love a bargain, and they will respect that your house is worth a certain amount. Be careful not to go too low or people may feel your property is inferior.

There are three primary things renters look for in a VR. First, they look for location, next they look at amenities, such as number of bedrooms and if it has a pool or fireplace, and third is price. This time, do a search for price and see what you come up with.

Take the lower price range and do a search for your same area. This time, broaden what you look at to include all VR's in the price point. For example, if you have a two bed, one bath condo on the beach, you may find the same money gets you a four bed, three bath house three blocks inland. It's important to know what your competition is in terms of location, amenities, and price. This helps you sell your property as a winning rental.

When people say, "I can get another property for $200 a night," you are in a position to talk about the benefits of your property. The reverse is true, if someone calls and mentions that another property is beachfront, and yours is not, you can talk about the value of saving hundreds of dollars by booking yours. Knowledge is powerful.

As you conduct your search, pretend that you are searching for a vacation. If your price point is $200/night, for example, see what you can get for the money.

Same Price Comparable #1

How is it different?

_____

_____

_____

_____

_____

_____

Comparable #2
How is it different?

_____

_____

_____

_____

_____

Comparable # 3
How is it different?

_____

_____

_____

_____

_____

Homework

Now that you've looked at the competition, be brutally honest about your house. How does it measure up? If you couldn't find any vacation rentals in your area, that's either a really good thing or a really bad thing. Does your area attract vacationers? If not, do the locals need a place to house extra guests? Is it possible that it would work better as a long-term rental? Does the market seem saturated with VR's?

Chapter 7
Property Management Company or DIY?

Chapter Summary

- Skill Set Needed to Successfully Run a Vacation Rental
- Discover Your Unique Skill Set
- Property Management Companies

Which is more important to you, money or freedom? Here lies the answer of whether to hire a property management company or do it yourself. If you manage your property yourself, then following the practices laid out in this book will create higher sales and a greater income than if you hire a management company. But if your life is pulling at you at both ends, and you don't have time to do what's already on your plate, a property management company may be the best way to go. Another important factor to consider is whether your total costs before hiring someone will allow you to make a profit if you add the extra expense of a management company. If not, this book will direct you towards success.

Skill Set Needed to Successfully Run a Vacation Rental

Marketing Io oimply getting the word out. Let potential renters know about your property. VR marketing is primarily internet driven, which makes it easy for both owner and renter to connect.

Choose avenues to use that will bring solid leads and sales. Go with 3-5 listing portals. Three obvious choices with proven track records are FlipKey, HomeAway, and VRBO. New to FlipKey and want to try them out? Go to www.FlipKey.com/list and when you finish filling out the form, enter "VRFUSION" in the coupon line. You will get 60 days free, plus $50 off your first year.

A simple, photo driven business website will round out your marketing efforts. It's just that easy. See Chapter 15. The best owners/managers do a market analysis—that is, carefully comparing costs of other VR rentals in your area to determine your price point. If you did your homework in the last chapter, you should be well prepared.

Sales - If the word "Sales" sends shivers down your spine, you may have found the one sales job that will be perfect for you. You don't have to go door to door or make cold calls. No pressuring someone into something they don't want. People actually come to you, hungry for more information and to reserve their vacation.

No one is a better sales person for your home than you—you loved it enough to buy it. No property management company can come close to your passion for your home. But, if talking on the phone is intimidating to you, or if e-mails will simply go unanswered, which is never acceptable, you may want to consider a property management company. Property management companies are usually skilled at sales as they work on commission.

The job of sales doesn't simply end with a check deposited or credit card number processed. There are a few simple tasks that will ensure that you don't double book. After you close the sale and collect information from the guest, you'll need to block the dates on the calendar, process the payment, and record the details of the sale. If they didn't pay in full, you will follow up with final payment, then send a Welcome Packet by e-mail or snail mail.

You must be organized and detail oriented or you will end up with various calamities like double bookings, over or under billing, or a guest not knowing how to check into your home. It is not as difficult as it might appear; it simply requires you to have a system in place to be sure everything on the list is complete. Once again, if it is too much you can hire a management company to take care of your bookings for you. It is far better to do that then have the constant stress of worrying about if you have all your tasks complete for the reservation.

Basic Accounting- If you have only one or two VR's, accounting can be easy. It's a matter of keeping things simple. I take a deposit of 30 percent of the total amount, then the final payment is due thirty days prior to arrival. A quick look at the calendar tells me who to send a reminder e-mail to next. In the notes section of the calendar program, I put the total sale, the deposit made, and the balance due. When it's time for final payment, which happens about every week to ten days, I simply looks back in the notes section.

$1500-500=1000

The above sample note tells me that the total price of the booking was $1500, the guests paid a deposit of $500, leaving a final balance of $1000. Thirty days prior to their arrival, I send a final payment notice of $1000 due. Easy!

Sandra's sixteen properties require a simple spreadsheet, but are still at the "Do It Yourself" level.

Record keeping for tax purposes- You will have various expenses you can deduct from your taxes. Keep all receipts together in order to provide complete information to your accountant. Check with your accountant beforehand to see what is deductible. Linens, silverware, marketing, and even your own travel expenses can be legitimate business expenses. As the rules can be difficult to navigate, be sure you have an accountant. If you do not self-manage, your property manager will have a complete record of the expenses incurred throughout the year that you can submit to your accountant.

Of course, if the home is more for your own private use, and you only rent it to friends on occasion, it might not meet the standards of being a business. Again, money spent on an accountant is money well spent. Make sure to get one that is experienced in vacation rentals to make sure you are taking your full deductions, but not more.

Purchasing - Do you like to shop? Do you love a great bargain? You will need to purchase a variety of different items for your home. Linens will get stained, forks will accidentally get thrown away, and towels will get holes in them. Your guests expect the same quality of linens they would find in a hotel. If you are a $70/night VR, then you may be able to buy inexpensive linens. If you are a $250/night operation, you'll need to up the quality. However, the quality is what the guests notice, not the price tag. If you can find 600 thread count, Egyptian cotton sheets at Overstock for $69, and another store is selling them for $229, get them at Overstock. Every penny that you save on purchasing affects your bottom line.

Quality Control -Feedback from your guests is very important, but they might not tell you the sheets have a tear or that there is a leak under the sink in the bathroom. It's important to have someone on site who can make sure the property is well maintained from the gutters to the dishes. Your housekeeper or property manager can spot check and pass the information on to you.

Customer Service-Someone has to take the calls when guests have a question or have a need. To cut down on the number of calls, give a clear picture in your marketing of what your property actually is. Then, construct a comprehensive Welcome Packet and Guest Information Book. Label things well, and make sure the items are where they are supposed to be during cleans. If you or your housekeeper can't find the remote, chances are, neither will the guest. Spell out as much as you can in your Guest Information Book so they can find the answer without having to call you.

If you employ a management company they will be the ones to provide the customer service to your guest. Give them a test run to see how they respond to different situations before you hire them to ensure the best quality customer service is given to your guest.

Housekeeping- Great housekeepers make your VR look as if your current guests are the first to ever stay there. Unless you are very detail oriented and are a great cleaner and enjoy staging, this is something to consider hiring out. However, if you live nearby and enjoy the process of preparing the property to welcome new guests, doing it yourself is a way to increase your income. One owner who "pays" herself for each clean she does. That's her travel fund, and it adds up quickly when you have more than one property.

Maintenance-Most of us don't have enough maintenance knowledge to fix everything that breaks. Finding a go-to maintenance person or company is essential. Don't wait until you have a problem. Interview a few people, and keep their names and numbers stored in your phone. When a problem arises, and it will, it will likely be at 10:00 on a Friday night. You will feel very organized if all you have to do is call someone you have already met and who has seen the house. Of course, in the interview, you'll ask if they do after-hours calls. Expect to pay a premium. It's worth it. Angie's List, www.angieslist.com , is a good source for maintenance contacts. You may even know someone who is a handyman who can help out. If your VR is part of a condo, they may have their own people. Make sure to take care of your maintenance people, they will save the day for you!

Landscaping-If your VR has a yard, landscaping is something that will have to be taken care of, either by you or someone you hire. Condo owners often have that taken care of as part of their association fees.

Vacation rental management usually isn't an all or nothing deal. While I manage marketing, sales basic accounting and off-site customer service at Starfish Blue in Fiji, as a remote owner, I am limited with how hands-on I can be. On the ground, I have a team of 4 people who handle customer service, record keeping, maintenance, and housekeeping. Because labor is so inexpensive in Fiji, I can affordably provide jobs for several people. I have two maids, a manager, and a pool man/landscaper, all who work a few hours a day.

Discover Your Unique Skill Set

Consider your unique skill set. Where are your strengths? Weaknesses? One couple might be a dynamite team for housekeeping and maintenance, but struggle with marketing and sales. Be realistic about what you're great at, what you can do, and what needs to be hired out. Answer the following questions as a strength or weakness to assess if you should consider hiring the particular task out or do it yourself.

Marketing
~Are you computer savvy?
~Can you write a good description of your property and location?
~Are you good at taking photos?
~Can you comparison shop (market analysis) to set your price point?

Sales

~Do you like to talk about your property and the location it is in with enthusiasm?

~Do you have enough time to answer e-mails and calls in a timely manner?

~Are you detail oriented- able to keep an accurate calendar of guests?

~Are you detail oriented- able to keep accurate records of deposits, final payments due, and deposits returned?

Basic Accounting

~Do you like math?

~Are you detail oriented?

~Do you pay your bills on time?

Record Keeping

~Do you enjoy keeping up with receipts?

~Do you like creating order?

~Do you enjoy details?

Purchasing (Shopping)

~Do you like to shop?

~Do you have an eye for a bargain?

~Do you have an eye for style and design?

Quality Control

~Do you notice the smallest detail?

~Do you make needed changes quickly?

Customer Service

~Do you feel strongly about giving good service?

~Do you like interfacing with people?

~Will you get defensive with a complaint, or will you be able to distance yourself?

Housekeeping

~Do you like to clean?

~Do you mind seeing your house a mess?

~Are you detail oriented?

Maintenance

~Do you have basic plumbing skills?

~Do you have basic carpentry skills?

~Do you have basic electrical skills?

~Do you like to figure out why something isn't working?

~Can you follow the directions in a basic repair hand book?

~Do you own tools to make simple repairs?

Property Management Companies

After evaluating your skill set, does it look like a property management company is the best option for you? If so, do your research carefully and interview a few companies to make sure you are working with the best of the best. Some companies offer a hybrid relationship, where you can handle sales and marketing, and they handle payment, check in, housekeeping, and any issues that arise during your guests' stay. Even if you don't get an additional percentage for booking your own property, which some companies do offer, you will certainly offer better knowledge of your property to prospective guests if you do marketing in addition to what the PM company offers.

Check reviews of homes that are managed by property management companies you are considering. Do guests seem happy with the customer service experience? Talk to other owners. Ask for occupancy rates. This is a relationship you will likely be in for a minimum of a year, so you want it to be a good fit.

When you have it narrowed down to one or two companies, it's a good idea to go the extra step of booking a short stay with them. If you have time, two short stays will give you much better insight into how they run their company. Do one booking over the phone and another via email. What's the response time? Do they answer all of your questions? Is the process arduous? Do they care about their guests? Call with a question during your stay and gauge the response.

While many people are quite capable of renting their home out themselves, for some people, the best alternative is a property management company. However, if you have the time, being an involved owner will make your property stand out from the pool of listings. No one knows your property like you do, so use the tips in this book to write your own copy, take stunning photos, and have a web site that offers area information and a personal touch. Read on for decorating and organizing tips for the guests' benefit, and for amenities that can give your home the wow factor that will leave people happy. And who knows, you might be able to get involved and help with a cranky guest, and leave the customer with a positive view after a negative experience. Being involved in many areas, such as checking your listing for accuracy and making sure your home has what it needs, can get you more bookings, which is good for everyone.

Homework

Now that you've taken a realistic look at what you bring to the table, what areas will you handle the work yourself, and what areas will you hire out? If you are a couple or group going into this endeavor, divide up the areas of responsibility in writing.

	DIY	Hire Out	Notes
Marketing			
Sales			
Basic Accounting			
Record Keeping			
Purchasing			
Quality Control			
Customer Service			
Housekeeping			
Maintenance			

Chapter 8
How to Choose and Work with a Property Manager

Covered in this chapter

- Benefits of Having a Property Manager
- Where to Look for a Good Property Management Company
- Questions to Ask While Interviewing the Company
- How to Develop a Good Working Relationship

Let's be realistic, some of us don't have time to spend on managing our vacation home or maybe you don't have a desire to. If you fall into either of these categories hiring a property manager to take care of your VR is a good choice. Once you have made the decision to go with a property management company the next questions are where do you find one and how do you choose one out of the vast array available.

Benefits of Having a Property Manager

There are many benefits to having a property manager. Obviously, they will free up time answering phone calls, replying to e-mail inquiries, taking reservations, and managing the billing and deposits. Beyond those fundamentals you will be able to piggyback your personal marketing strategies on top of the management company's, drawing more prospective guests to view your property.

Consider the stress burden that will be lifted from your day to day life. There will be no phone call to be answered by you at 2:00 a.m. that the furnace has gone out or your guest has accidentally locked themselves out of the home. Your management team will have someone on call to take care of those concerns. They should periodically check on your property during off-season, inspecting to be sure nothing looks out of the ordinary, giving you peace of mind that all is well. A good management company will have staff that will be doing preventative maintenance, keeping your property in the best possible condition while identifying and dealing with repair needs before they become a major expense.

Your property manager should have a list of credible service providers—all of whom have been researched to be fully insured, bonded, and licensed. The leg work is done ahead of time making sure you have a service provider that has fair pricing and whose work is up to code.

Having a company that keeps up with your costs, receipts, and income generated is a relief if you are not detail oriented. Your management team should generate monthly reports with detailed documentation of all costs, revenue generated, and room and state tax's that were paid. All you have to do is print the report off and put it in a file for tax season. Easy. Some provide an annual report structured for tax purposes and advise you on relevant tax deductions.

Where to Find a Good Property Management Company

If you own a condo in a large complex you may not have a choice as to who manages your property. It is often taken care of by an in-house company. If you own a home or have the flexibility of choosing outside of your condo group there are a few good ways to find a reputable management company. VRMA (Vacation Rental Management Association) is a good place to start. Management companies who are members have the most current information on industry trends and practices. You can also speak to other VR owners in your area. See who they recommend as property management and who they believe you should avoid. On VRBO and HomeAway you can now see on the dashboard who works with property managers and who self-manages. Pick up a vacation rental magazine from your area and see who advertises in it. Google vacation rentals in your area and see what companies come up in the top five. From those suggestions you should be able to generate a list with at least three or four companies that look worthy of further investigation.

Questions to Ask While Interviewing the Company

After generating your list of perspective property managers, the next step is to contact the company itself. Send an e-mail inquiry on a random property managed by them to see how quickly it is responded to, if they answer questions fully, give you the complete cost of your stay, and tell you how to reserve. Make a phone inquiry as well gathering the same information. You may be able to eliminate candidates off the list at this point if the inquiry response was not handled properly.

With your short list in hand, phone up the manager of the company and make an appointment to interview them. The following is a list of questions you will want to ask:

MARKETING

Is there a set-up fee? This can range from $0 to $500 and up to cover efforts and costs for marketing.

What are your company's marketing strategies? Listing portals? Mail Outs? E-mail blasts? Vacation magazines? Who pays for the marketing?

Am I able to add to those strategies with my own additional marketing?

Am I able to maintain a personal website for my property linked to you for reservations?

How do you determine rates and fees?

RESERVATIONS

How do you handle reservations?

How are deposits handled? When are they returned to the guest?

Who keeps pet fees, cleaning fees, or any additional fees?

CUSTOMER SERVICE

How do you handle customer complaints?

Who is responsible for any charge backs or fees associated with them?

What is guest check in and check out procedure?

How are keys handled? Who on your staff will have keys to my property?

What if friends or family want to stay? Is there a charge for handling keys and maintenance calls during non-paying guests' stays?

MAINTENANCE

How are maintenance concerns handled?

How am I billed for maintenance at my property?

Is there regular preventative maintenance done?

Can maintenance handle yard work, snow, and leaf removal?

Who takes care of trash pick-up?

Will my property be checked on during times of no occupancy?

Do you have a list of service providers for large maintenance issues who you regularly use? Are they licensed, bonded, and insured? Has their work been checked for quality or code standards? Has their price been compared? Can I choose to use a provider outside of your group?

HOUSEKEEPING

Tell me about housekeeping staff.

Do you have a check list I can see of tasks they are to complete during a routine cleaning?

Do you do seasonal cleans wiping baseboards, washing windows etc.?

If a guest complains of a theft by housekeeping how would it be handled?

What is your turnover rate for housekeeping?

Who pays for housekeeping? Does housekeeping work by the hour or by the clean?

Who inspects to be sure the property was properly cleaned?

CONTRACTS / FEES / REPORTING

What provisions are made for termination?

May I see a sample contract?

Can you identify all potential fees for me? (All fees are negotiable.) What services are included in those fees?

Are fees billed or deducted from my account?

Must I keep additional funds in an account for emergency repairs?

What day of the month do I get paid? Can you do direct deposit?

What type of monthly report will you send me? Does it include a detailed breakdown of income and itemized expenses? Can I see a sample copy of one?

What do I do if I have a dispute?

Do you provide annual reporting structured for tax purposes?

REFERENCES

Can you provide me with some references?

YOUR OWN QUESTIONS

1._____

2._____

3._____

Once you have completed the interview process and checked the references you should have a very good idea of which company will best meet your needs. Remember to consider the "personality" of the company, making sure it is a good fit with yours.

How to Develop a Good Working Relationship

Now that you have found the perfect company to manage your property you will want to work on developing a strong working relationship with them. You don't want to be overly involved—give them space to do their job—but you do want to follow up, spot checking the cleanliness of the property at times and following up with guests occasionally that have stayed in your home.

Take time to develop a relationship with the staff, letting them know you appreciate what they do to take care of your home. Get to know them on a first name basis and take time to talk with them when you see them. If they know who you are and you appreciate the work they do they will likely continue to work hard to keep your property in its best condition and that your guests receive high quality guest services. Remember, these are the people who have charge of one of your largest assets and will be making decisions on your behalf; you want to have a positive relationship with them.

Homework

Take time to reconsider all of the positives of having a property manager. Make it personal to you and your given circumstances, don't simply list the positives mentioned in the chapter above. Yes, you will likely have fewer bookings and there is a cost to have someone do the work for you, but money may not be a dominant factor in why you have decided not to self- manage.

_____

_____

_____

_____

Go back to this list when you are questioning if you should continue with a property manager. It is easy to forget all the work that goes into managing your own VR. This will help you remember why you made the choice you did and reevaluate if it was a good one in a year's time.

Chapter 9
Policies and Contracts

Covered in this Chapter

- Fragmented Industry
- Evaluate the Market
- Responding to Inquiries
- Marking Your Calendar
- Establishing Policies
- Creating Your Contract

Fragmented Industry

PhoCusWright did a study of the VR Industry, and while they discovered a plethora of positive things, one of the criticisms of the industry is that we are fragmented. It's true.

Hotels, resorts, and cruises all have fairly similar practices. If you reserve a hotel, you can usually see live availability online, reserve with a credit card, and receive an immediate confirmation. It can take less than ten minutes.

Since the vacation rental industry, particularly the individually owned and marketed properties, is relatively new to the travel industry, booking a vacation rental can be an arduous task. HomeAway and VRBO are leading the way in making the reservation system much more streamlined with online reservations, billing, and contracts through their sites. There are numerous smaller companies that offer this reservation service for a fee. They range from simple to very high tech including emarketing and developing reports for your property. Consider looking into these options. It can make the job of customer management so much easier, as well as making the task of finding and booking a rental an easy, quick process for your guests.

Within the VR industry, there are acceptable norms. In some areas of the world, there are no cleaning fees. I offer free, daily maid service. It's a viable option because the price of labor is inexpensive, and I am able to provide jobs and contribute back to the community. In many areas, cleaning fees are the norm, as is asking guests to start a load of laundry, take out the trash, and clear out the refrigerator. Both of these approaches are acceptable.

What is not a good business practice is to ask the guest to clean the house. Make sure your policies are available to your guests, either on your website or in your lease agreement, before they pay. Some guests absolutely do not want to do any cleaning, and this would be a rude shock to them if they were not made aware of it ahead of time.

Evaluate the Market

Look at the norms in your area. Just because everyone else does it, doesn't mean it's a good idea for your business. In some areas of the world, most of the VR's run by property management companies require a week's stay that starts on a Saturday or Sunday, charge a linen fee of about $100, a cleaning fee, and a reservation fee of over $100. So, when you see a condo listed for $900, you are likely going to spend

$1700, once you have added the fees and taxes. Do you see any opportunities to separate yourself from the pack?

You can look at all of those policies and see if any of them are necessary. You could actually do better than the market average, by having policies that are good for customers. An enterprising owner could capitalize on this concept; "Stay when you want for as long as you want. No hidden fees. Linens provided at no extra charge." That would grab the attention of many travelers.

My family and I vacation in the Outer Banks. As a VR owner, I was startled by the numerous upcharges that were standard across the island chain. I felt these should have been absorbed into the cost of the rental- so you are comparing apples to apples and know what your cost will be without a lot of hassle and research. Our first vacation there, I actually bought linens at Walmart (for the bed sizes we didn't have) rather than pay $100 for a one week linen rental.

The second year, I sought out a vacation rental that didn't have the additional fees.

While the VR culture of the Outer Banks and other places have supported fees and extra charges, as people get used to using VR's for all of their travel, they will expect industry norms. This is a real opportunity for savvy VR owners.

Responding to Inquiries

As an owner or manager, you should strive to answer your e-mails immediately. Some owners look at an e-mail, find out their calendar is full, and do not answer. This is terrible for business. It's rude to your perspective guest and makes all vacation rental owners look unprofessional.

On HomeAway's new system owners can pre-enter a generic response, one for reserved, one for available. As long as you keep up with your free calendar on their system, when an inquiry arrives in your inbox, there is a note that says whether your property is available or not. With one click, you can send the appropriate response. They can hear back from you in one minute if you have a smart phone or are at your computer.

Once potential guests have established a rapport with you, they are unlikely to switch to another owner who responds much later. They see you as an involved owner, one who values them.

Marking Your Calendar: The Mark of a Professional

Keeping up with your calendar is a mark of a professional. How would you feel if you tried to reserve the Marriott, and when you looked on their website, it showed a range of options, from king, to 2 queens, to smoking, to handicapped. But when you tried to make a reservation, you find it's completely sold out. It would make most people frustrated. Yet, many, many owners do the same thing.

Some do it out of laziness or being too busy, some do it out of disregard, some do it in hopes of talking the guest into staying at another time.

We suggest going with only three to five listing portals because it's easier to keep up the calendars on fewer websites. Make it part of your sales routine, before you run their credit card or accept their check, complete their reservation by blocking the dates on the calendar. Then, send them an e-mail with confirmation, and tell them their vacation is now live on your calendar. It's another step in making their dream a reality.

If you can't keep up with this part of the reservation process, it's time to look at a property management company.

Establishing Policies

Renting your home is a business. Some owners have a conversation with each guest, trying to conduct a phone interview. While many owners have never had a problem with guests causing damage, if you are in an area where people come to party, you may need to establish upfront guidelines.

Check with your lawyer to see what's legal. A high deposit is a good way to off-set fees from damage and it gives people an incentive to treat your home well. This can, however, if disputed, lead to legal issues. Make sure to document everything well.

Some owners have a minimum age rental, and require all guests to submit a photo ID and sign the contract. I have a one page lease agreement with one signature required and do not keep a deposit. The few items that have been broken, like a blender and a rice cooker, are a part of doing business. I want to keep the happy feeling of booking in their mind, and the lease agreement is a simple document, outlining the few rules, such as no smoking inside the house, and the cancellation policy.

Sandra has a rather lengthy contract that must be initialed throughout and signed at the bottom. She does not take a deposit having it stated in her contract that if need be she has permission to bill the credit card on file for any damage. This can be risky as the guest may dispute the charge with the credit card company.

When a guest disputes a charge you must be prepared with detailed documentation, photographs, and a signed contract to have any hope of winning the case and keeping the money owed for damage. Often the card company will still side with the card holder regardless of documentation. Different locations require different standard contracts because of the types of guests they attract. Try to find what is normal in your area.

Besides a contract there are other policies you will want to consider having in place. You can list these on your website or have them documented in your rental agreement.

Smoking: It is common for most Vacation Rental homes to be smoke-free but it is your home and entirely your choice. You can allow guest to smoke outside in designated areas but be sure those are clearly defined in your policy and Guest Information Book. As people have allergies to smoke, if you promote your property as smoke free, it is fair to impose an additional cleaning fee to people who violate the rule. Have that clearly defined in your lease agreement.

Pets: It is becoming more and more common for guests to travel with their pets. If you choose to be pet friendly state your specific guidelines on the issue clearly on your website and contract. Sandra has all guests send her a photo copy of the flea and tick medications the animal is on to prevent an infestation. She also specifies that pets are not to be left unattended unless they are properly crated and no pets are ever allowed on bedding or furnishings. She states the damage fee if any evidence is found that the guest with a pet has disregarded the policy.

As Fiji is an international destination, I've only had one request to bring a pet. They understood when I told them I couldn't accommodate their request, as our staff would have to be completely trained on cleaning after a pet. They left the dog at home and had a wonderful stay.

Check Out Procedure- Carefully outline what, if anything, you expect your guests to do upon check out. If their idea of a vacation involved packing their clothes and leaving, this is the time to let them know you expect them to strip the beds, take out the garbage, and wash the dishes.

Cancelation policy: This policy needs to be stated on your listing portal, website, and in your contract. Spell this out for your guest so there is no misunderstanding. It is common to have a thirty-day prior to stay cancellation. Should a guest cancel for any reason within thirty days they forfeit the entire amount. Prior to thirty days the guest forfeits a $100 processing fee.

Trip Insurance Clause- Encourage your guests to consider trip insurance at time of reservation. This prevents a guest calling days before a stay and saying they must cancel and plead for their money back. Since the cancellation policy is clearly outlined in your guest lease, as is the encouragement to purchase trip insurance, it takes the responsibility off you when a guest asks for a refund. Simply remind them of the trip insurance clause, and offer to write a letter to the trip insurance company outlining your cancellation policy.

I have had a few guests who have had to cancel, for death in the family, an ear infection which prevented flying, or a serious illness. On each occasion, when the guests have purchased insurance, the company promptly sends the guest a refund. If they have not purchased the policy it is their burden.

Payment: Most VR's charge a deposit that is applied directly to the guest balance at time of reservation. The remaining balance is typically billed thirty days prior to stay. Some bill out sixty days prior to stay.

It is also common to charge an additional security deposit ranging from $100 to $300. Some houses, such as multi-bedroom, beachfront homes which will serve more than one family can charge $1,000 and up. The deposit is to be returned after guest departure and an inspection of the property.

Minimum age and maximum guests to stay on property: You may want to specify a minimum age for guests renting your property. Depending on where you are located and the type of guests that frequent the area you can decide on a reasonable age. Most common is age twenty-one, but if your home is in a location that is a favorite vacation spot for college students on spring or winter break you might want to consider age twenty-five.

Number of Guests- You will also need to clearly define how many guests are appropriate to stay in your property. This is for a number of reasons; you don't want your lovely home to become party central and have items broken or missing. You also don't want four families vacationing together in your three bedroom two bath home, the septic will not be able to handle it and again it will produce significant wear and tear on your property.

Rules- Guests need to know what's expected of them. Do they have parking restrictions, pool rules to follow, noise levels to adhere to?

Being a good neighbor is an important part of running your business, unless you own a secluded cabin. Always consider your neighbors. Respect their privacy and their right to the quiet enjoyment of their own property. They can be your eyes and ears when you are away.

While noise hasn't been an issue in Fiji, as landlord of long term properties in Asheville, I screen carefully for noise. We have lovely apartments with large decks and year round mountain views. Our tenants love to sit out on their decks and watch the sunset in the evenings. It's a peaceful way to end a long day at the office. I have a clause in the lease that says if the police are called for noise violation and a citation is written, the tenant can and will be evicted. Keeping the other tenants happy takes priority over one tenant. If these units were VR's, I would market them as "quiet and peaceful" and put the same clause in the lease.

If your second home is in an area of loud vacationers, good neighbor relations are critical. As more and more counties are outlawing VR's, as owners, we need to do everything we can to keep our neighbors happy- if they are unhappy, they will let local government know about it. Be a good neighbor and let your guests know the rules, and let your neighbors know that you value them. It would not be fun to live next to a house where guests left garbage all over the lawn, parked on the grass, and partied until 4 AM. Give them your contact information and tell them it won't offend you if they call the police on rowdy renters. Show them your lease and ask for input.

Minimum stay: If you have contracted with a management company you may not have an option for taking less than a week long stay. If you are able to manage yourself you are open to being more flexible. It is usually cost effective to have a three night minimum up to a week stay. You might want to consider an additional fee for booking less than the minimum stay.

Month long or extended stays: You will probably get requests for month long stays, especially in the off-season. People have come to expect deep discount. Some things to consider- how high will your utilities be? In Fiji, the low season is actually our most expensive time for utilities, as it's hot and humid during the rainy season. In other areas, heating costs would be an issue, especially if your home is not well insulated. When you factor in any addition costs (will you have to plow the driveway if it snows?) consider how many days renting at normal rate would you need to equal the discounted rate.

Another thing to consider is to make sure you haven't legally switched from short term to long term. Or if you have, that you understand the ramifications and what that does to your state and local tax (generally, long term renters do not pay any tax- so you want to make sure you don't collect tax when it's not due.) In many areas, the line between short term and long term stays are 30, 60, or 90 days.

81

Holidays- It's common to have a special policy for holidays- a higher rate and a minimum stay. If your normal minimum is 2 nights, you might be able to secure a reservation for 5 or 7 nights over Christmas, New Years, and Easter. Country specific holidays, as well as spring break are common times to increase your minimum stay.

Creating Your Contract

Just as hiring an accountant is a requirement for any business, I highly recommend enlisting the services of a lawyer to make sure that you are following all of the local, state, and national laws, as well as protecting yourself. It should take no more than an hour or two of a lawyer's time to draw up a short term lease agreement.

Try to avoid long contracts. My vision has always been that we should do everything a hotel does, only better, and hotels don't have any contracts, so my lease agreement is friendly and one page. Yet, Sandra's contract is lengthier as she feels it important to protect herself and her assets. Somewhere between a one and five page contract is a good balance. The bottom line is have a contract that your guest signs giving you permission to bill their credit card (if you bill in that manner), the dates they will be checking in and out, how many will be in the party, and the total rates and fees due and when.

To avoid the hassle of printing, mailing, faxing, scanning, and attaching, look for a company that allows you to do this online. HomeAway has recently come out with a free product where if you use their company for credit card processing, you can upload your contract and have HomeAway handle all guest paperwork management for you. At the time of this writing, there is no monthly fee, no commission, only a 2.5 percent credit card processing fee, which is very reasonable. It's worth looking into. Some owners are concerned about a listing portal having all of the information on their guests, so this is something you may want to research further.

Homework

Check your area for normal VR policies. Are there age restrictions? Smoking Policies? Additional Fees? Are taxes included? Do a little detective work and find out what the norm is for your area.

_____
_____
_____
_____
_____
_____
_____
_____
_____
_____

Which policies do you agree with? Why?

_____
_____
_____
_____
_____
_____
_____

Which ones would you change in your business? Why?

_____
_____
_____
_____
_____
_____

Chapter 10
Long Distance Management

Covered in this chapter

- Quiz—Do You Have What it Takes to be a Long Distance Manager?
- Setting Up Your Home
- Finding Great Staff
- Training Your Staff
- Creative Ways to Show Your Staff What Guests Expect
- Backup Plan

Many owners who live away from their vacation rental do not consider management a viable option. They hand over the keys to a property management company without exploring the alternatives. Some owners are able to work out a hybrid situation in which they handle sales, and the management company handles things on the ground.

A property management company may be the best situation. But, if you have the time and inclination to manage it yourself, no one will be a better sales person and advocate than you. You are the owner. It is not always easy, but it is very doable.

Quiz—Do you have what it takes to be a long distance manager?

Take this quiz. The more "Yes" answers, the more able you are to manage long distance successfully.

Y   N   Do you have enough time to set things in motion (furnish house, if needed, set up listings online, take photos or videos, etc.)?

Y   N   Will you be able to visit your vacation rental a minimum of once a year?

Y   N   Do you have twenty minutes a day to devote to e-mails?

Y N   Do you have one to two additional hours a week, as needed?

Y N   Are you passionate about your vacation rental and its location?

Y   N   Can you find someone you trust to be your manager at the property?

Y   N   Can you provide tools for them to do their job effectively?

Y   N   Are you willing to continue to train, train, train your staff until they fully understand and your expectations?

Y   N   Are you willing to treat your staff well and with respect?

Write down the obstacles you're concerned about.

_____
_____
_____
_____
_____
_____

Setting Up Your Home

Initially, unless you purchase an existing home or new build that is furnished, it will take time to set up the vacation rental yourself. In remote locales, like islands and third world nations, this can be a huge expense and you might not get it decorated the way you want. Keep in mind that simple is better when it comes to décor.

Finding Great Staff

Once the house is ready, you'll need someone to be your representative on the ground. Key qualities are:

- Good communication skills
- Trustworthy
- Truthful
- Excellent customer service skills
- A deep understanding and appreciation for guests' expectations
- Contacts locally to get things fixed fast
- Backup plan in place

Let's talk about these. For remote ownership, we are going to include and consider issues that overseas owners have. Not all of this will apply if you live in Michigan and have a home in Florida, but some will. You might, one day, decide to own a home in Belize, so read on!

Good communication skills

It is necessary to be able to speak the same language. If your home is in Mexico, it's great if you speak Spanish. However, it's likely that most of your guests will not. So you need to find someone that you and your guests can communicate with easily. The more fluent your manager is in English (or the language that you and your guests speak) the better the fit for the job.

Part of communication will involve technology. I had a potential manager for my home in Fiji. This woman was hardworking, spoke excellent English, excelled in customer service, and worked for me for a number of years as a maid. She understood what the clients wanted and took a lot of pride in her job. She went over and above what was expected, like making an inventory of linens, etc. But this woman didn't have electricity. This meant no fax, no e-mail, and no cell phone. Logistically, it would have been a nightmare. If she had electricity, I could have gotten her a laptop and cell phone. But, there was also no door to her house. It's likely the items would have been stolen. I had to look at the whole picture.

It's best to have two means of communication with your manager; phone, whether a landline, cell phone, satellite phone, or Skype, is essential. Essential. They have to hear the passion in your voice when you are trying to express a foreign concept to them. If there is a complaint, you need to be able to get through to them exactly what the problem was—to make sure they not only understand the idea for that one instance, but for the broader concept.

If there is a language barrier, there is likely a cultural barrier, as well. It can take years of training and grooming to develop the high standards that you expect.

Excellent Customer Service Skills

In some parts of the world, an emphasis is placed on placating an upset person rather than solving the problem. Promises are made with no intention of being kept, pretty white lies are told to cover an ugly truth, and guests are left with nothing to show for their frustrations except for empty words.

If you are working with a different culture, you are likely trying to move a boulder uphill to get this to move. But, it will move. It's just going to take more effort. And if you find your staff is not getting just how important customer service is, you need to find someone else. This is YOUR business.

With my first management team, a husband and wife, I noticed a lethargy to guests' concerns. No amount of talking or faxing would convince them that it was in everyone's best interest for them to deal with a problem immediately or try to avoid one. After a particularly negative e-mail, in which the guests had valid complaints, an idea struck. I constructed a very compelling fax (this was before my new manager, who has e-mail).

Steve, you are the house manager. If there is a problem, it is your job to fix it. If the guests are unhappy with something on the grounds or in the house, it is your job. You are the manager. (Before he was the caretaker. See the shift?)
Sally, you are the guest manager. If the guests are lacking something or have a need, it is your job to fix it. It is your job to make sure they have what they need to have a wonderful holiday.
To show you how important this is, I am going to give you FJD$25 for every e-mail I get from guests where they say what a wonderful time they had. I will not count it against you if the refrigerator breaks, only if it breaks and it is not dealt with quickly.

Guess what? I started getting e-mails raving about Steve and Sally. With their newfound confidence and incentive, they established a rapport with the guests. Almost immediately, emails started coming in and they first thing they praised was the management team. In some cases, the highlight of the trip was when Steve and Sally (names changed) invited the guests over to their house for a home cooked meal. I have pages of e-mails praising Starfish Blue and the wonderful staff, Steve and Sally. And that is the best USD$15/guest I could ever spend.

This also gave them more standing in the community. They were no longer the maid and the caretaker, they were managers. You can't promote someone above their abilities, but in this instance, it worked like a charm.

A deep understanding of guests' expectations

Often, the people working for you won't live or vacation to the same standard that your guests will. In some cases, there will be a huge disparity of their lifestyle and your home and your guests' expectations. Training is very important. While a ripped or stained sheet may seem like a luxury to a maid in a second world country, you have to let them know that everything has to be perfect. Just like out-of-the-package. They may not understand it the first time you tell them, or even the first ten times you tell them. In their minds, it's clean, serviceable, and better than what they have, and they are saving you the expense of buying new ones. This should be rewarded, but you have to educate them on guests' expectations.

Training Your Staff

One way to do this it to encourage them to look out for your best interest. Frugality is appreciated, but shift who is the "Boss" in their mind.

Say, *"I wouldn't mind sleeping with a sheet with a small rip in it, or using a towel that has a bleach stain. I'm with you. It's perfectly fine. However, you and I both work for the guest. And the guests, well, they are pickier than you and I are. They are paying extra for a special treat.*

So, we have to keep our bosses happy—all of the ones who come, week after week, to stay here. Can you help me by making sure everything is perfect?"

Guests are the driving force in our business, and the staff has to think of them as the ones they are trying to please, even more than you, the owner.

To emphasize this, I forward all guest feedback to the manager to share with the staff. When it's positive, I celebrate with them and encourage them. When there is a criticism, I point out how the reality fell short of the guests' expectations. In a follow up phone call, the onsite manager and I go over the difference between the guests expectation and the reality of the situation. We always make a plan for how to do better next time.

Feedback from your guests is like gold. If a guest alerts you to an issue; a leak under the sink, yard work started too early, rude staff, follow up on it immediately and thank them.

Creative Ways to Show your Employees What Guests Expect

Show them your website or listing. Point out the beautiful pictures. Tell them, "This is the picture the guests see. There are no stains or tears. When they get here, this is what they expect."

Magazines—show them magazines that depict the style of your vacation rental. Don't show them Southern Living if you have the clean lines of a downtown loft. Let them keep the magazines and go over them. Use it as a tool for their input.

If it's a magazine you love, with a style that fits your home, ask them, "What's your favorite photo?" Look at it together. Ask them questions to engage them and get them comfortable with it.

"What do you like about this?"

"How is this like our house?"

"How could we make our house more like this picture?"

Engage and encourage your staff. They are likely very intimidated by you—you are their boss and source of income. Look for ways to build them up and give them confidence. A confident staff member can deal with a leaky faucet, a lowly chamber maid cannot.

While you are there setting things up, set up appointments with contractors. Ask your manager for references, as there is often a complex network of friends and kickbacks, especially overseas.

My suggestion? Don't try to fight an entire culture's way of doing things. Work with it, and get involved in it. Have the plumber, carpenter, and electrician that your manager recommends over for tea or coffee. Get to know them a bit. Ask about their experience. And then tell them you feel confident the home is in good hands, and that you don't want your guests to be disappointed. Stress how important doing a good job at a fair price is. And hopefully, you'll have the beginning of a beautiful relationship with people who will care for your home while you are not there.

Back Up Plan

These are the best laid plans. But, things happen. A good manager solves problems, a great manager prevents problems. What are some problems you could foresee?

Manager is in the hospital
Keys are lost
Employee caught stealing
Clogged toilet
Guest needs a doctor
Water gets turned off for non-payment
Heating oil runs out in the middle of a guests' winter stay

And on and on. These things are rare, but it's good to have a plan and measures in place for preventing and dealing with problems that arise.

Homework

How will you encourage your staff to give your guests the best experience in your absence?

_____

_____

_____

_____

_____

_____

_____

What are some incentives you can give? Hint: praise, respect, and responsibility can be as important as money.

_____

_____

_____

_____

_____

_____

_____

_____

_____

_____

Chapter 11
Pet Friendly Properties

by Sandra Cloer

Covered in this chapter

- The Size and Scope of the Pet Market
- Things to Consider
- Market as Pet Friendly
- Pet Policy
- Pet Fees
- Pet Addendum
- Housekeeping
- Pet Friendly Special Amenities

Are you considering becoming pet friendly in your Vacation Rental? If you are, there is plenty to consider. It can be a fabulous way to broaden your client base and add an extra stream of revenue to your business, but being pet friendly comes with calculated risks so read on to see if choosing to accept pets as guests is a good business decision for you and your VR.

The Size and Scope of the Pet Market

According to the 2011-2012 National Pet Owners Survey 62 percent of American households own a pet. That equates into 72.9 million homes. That alone should cause you to sit up and take notice. Of those, 43 million own a dog. Talk about expanding your client base!

Let's break it down even further; $3.65 billion dollars is spent annually on boarding and grooming. Averaged out per house hold each pet owner spends $274 annually on boarding and $78 on travel with pets. Remember, that is an average. The number is significantly higher should you look to those households who are actually spending the money.

The hospitality industry has taken notice of the consistent growth in the pet market over the past ten years and is taking full advantage of the trend. You now find many hotels and VR's hanging a "Pets Welcome" sign. You don't have to search far to find hotels that are offering amenities we mere humans find quite luxurious. These special treats run the gamut from oversized plush doggie beds, doggie masseuses, gift baskets welcoming man's best friend with toys, treats and bones to keep the beloved pet occupied while the "parents" are out to dinner. One can even have doggie turn down, staff leaving biscuits on a freshly fluffed luxurious pillow bed for Rover!

According to the Travel Association of America, 49 percent of adult leisure travelers consider their pet to be part of their family. Eighteen percent of U.S. adult leisure travelers take their pets with them when they travel. Are you beginning to hear the "cha-ching" yet? Don't hear it? Okay, read on. According to PetRelcoation.com's Austin, Texas report in 2010 a majority of baby boomers named pet care and travel as *basic* needs, not luxury items. In looking at the growth statistics over the past ten years in the pet industry it seems to be one of the few industries that are "recession proof." I bet you hear the "cha-ching" now!

Things to Consider

Now that you are convinced that being pet friendly is a worthwhile endeavor let's discuss a few not so great things before putting down the pet welcome mat. According to studies published in *Journal of Allergy on Clinical Immunology*, *Scientific Journal of the American Academy of Allergy, Asthma and Immunology*, up to 10 percent of the general population has pet allergies. Of those, 40 percent are allergic to cats and dogs. Allergies to cats are twice as common as those who are allergic to dogs. The allergy is not typically to the fur or hair of the pet but the dander. Dander is the dry skin you find beneath the hair and is sloughed off regularly. There is no known breed of cat or dog that does not produce dander. Becoming pet friendly you may risk losing business to those who won't consider staying in a property that is pet friendly due to the risk of allergy flair up.

You will have extra wear and tear on your property. Dog claws can scratch hardwood floors and doors. Some pets can be destructive if left alone and not properly crated. You can put measures in place to be sure to the best of your ability that pets are not left unattended unless properly crated by including specific instructions in your rental agreement and taking an additional pet damage deposit to cover any costs of repair.

Male dogs may "mark" their new territory with their urine, unfortunately on the corners of your furniture. Small dogs are known to have accidents in the house. This doesn't seem to be a chronic issue for those who accept pets only occasionally, although you will certainly want to consider pet accidents and the cleaning and staining issue before making your final decision.

There will be extra housekeeping costs after a guest with a pet checks out. The house must be cleaned assuming that the next guest to check in has allergies. Some owners offset some of the additional cleaning time by making the guest with the pet responsible for a thorough vacuum before they depart. Never assume it will be cleaned properly by your guest, this is to simply cut the time down for housekeeping. Your pet fees will cover the additional thirty minutes to an hour of additional housekeeping costs.

There could be a flea infestation in your home causing you to cancel reservations and to close your property in order to treat it properly.

Sandra says: I had a guest check into a property and found fleas upon arrival. The current guests had no pets and neither had the previous. The fleas must have been left weeks prior. I was aghast, and quite frankly, so were my new guests! I treated them to a day out and properly fumigated the house, killing the fleas. Unfortunately, I still took a negative comment hit on a listing portal. I couldn't prove who brought the fleas in the house as they were likely from several guests past whose dog left the fleas to lay eggs. Once you have fleas you must treat the house for four weeks to be sure all the eggs and larva have been killed. It is expensive and in a worst case scenario, you may have to close the property for a week or longer for a very serious infestation.

Market as Pet Friendly

There are various listing portals for those who are offering pet friendly accommodations. One can search practically any place in the world to find just the right spot for you and man's best friend. These sites list hotels and VR's as well as pet friendly activities in the area including restaurants, parks, doggie day care, and vets. You can list your property for free on some, for a fee on others. A few of those sites are www.petfriendlytravel.com, www.bringfido.com, www.PetVR.com, www.dogfriendly.com, www.petswelcome.com. All major VR listing sites like HomeAway or Flip Key have you indicate if your property is pet friendly.

When taking photos of your property include a pet in some, maybe a guest on the porch having coffee with a dog snoozing nearby. Take pictures of water bowls in front of stores and restaurants on your Main Street showing your town is pet friendly. Go out on an adventure with your dog and have a companion take shots of you both on a hiking trail or throwing a ball on the beach. Those types of photos will catch your pet enthusiast's eye and draw them into your listing.

Write inviting copy for your listing on your portal site to help your guest envision themselves walking downtown with their pet or relaxing by a fire. List all of the area attractions that are pet friendly like dog parks, doggie day cares, trails, restaurants, shops, and any special events or festivals.

Pet Policy

The Pet Policy needs to be outlined on your website for guests to view before reserving. Include the total number of pets you will allow, age requirements, shots required, flea and tick treatments required, any special limits or restrictions (such as no pets on bedding or furniture), excessive barking rules, and the consequence for sneaking a pet in your home.

Pet Fees

People who travel with their pets are accustomed to being charged an additional fee for the privilege of bringing them into a property. It is not a necessity to charge a fee but let's face it, we are all in this to reduce our costs or make a profit, and charging a fee is standard. Pet fees range from $10 per evening per pet to $25 per evening per pet, maxing at $100 per pet per stay. Some VR owners assign a one time fee between $50 and $100 per stay. Research the going rate to kennel a pet or to hire a house sitter to care for the pet and fall someplace in the middle. Make sure your fee covers the extra costs you will pay housekeeping for the additional thirty minutes to an hour it will take to clean your home properly after a pet visits. Larger houses can take more time.

Use the pet fee as a point of negotiation to close a sale with a perspective guest who is on the fence about securing your property. Don't cut the fee too short, making sure you always cover the extra housekeeping costs.

There are guests traveling with tiny breeds. Some believe they should be exempt from pet fees because of their pet's size. You might want to consider reducing the fee a little if the guest is insistent, but you will still have the extra housekeeping costs regardless of the size of the pet. Pet dander is pet dander and it needs to be properly cleaned before the next guest arrives.

There is another type of guest who may request a reduction in fee, those with breeds that do not shed like poodles or terriers. Even though these breeds do not shed they still have pet dander and the potential to do damage. It is an added amenity to travel with a pet. Again, if a guest is requesting a reduction in fee use it as a point of negotiation to secure the reservation. You may want to consider reducing the fee some if you think you will lose the sale.

Occasionally, guests will try to sneak a pet in without paying a fee. Address the issue ahead of time in the policy section of your website and in the standard rental agreement the guest must sign and return to you. Note a fee for bringing an unapproved pet on property as well as the possibility of being asked to leave with no refund.

Pet damage deposits are entirely different from a pet fee. Deposits are a refundable fee ranging from $100 to $400 to cover any damage the pet might do while staying in your property. Deposits can be in addition to your pet fee or a stand-alone without charging a pet fee. Some owners do one or the other, some do both.

Pet Addendum

Just as was previously covered in your pet policy you will want to restate the requirements for having a pet on premises in detail. Have your guest initial it was read and agreed to in addition to the signature at the end of your general contract.

Here are some things you may wish to include in your pet addendum:

Vaccines required, flea and tick control required, pet to be properly crated when left alone on premises, pet to be properly leashed, owner to bag and dispose of pet waste, what type of extra cleaning guest must do on departure, if, how, and when a pet fee will be billed for additional cleaning or damage from pet, any pets to be excluded from stay (dangerous breeds, cats, birds etc.), owner assumes no responsibility for any pet illness, injury, or death of pet while on premises.

You may want to include more or less, depending on your given circumstances for your VR. For example, someone who owns a property in a rural county in Montana will likely not have leash or size restrictions for pets where someone renting out a beachfront condo will have both. Always check with your HOA to see what special requirements they have for pets before you develop your Pet Addendum.

The following example of a Pet Addendum is provided by HomeAway and is available in a free download at www.community.HomeAway.com. After you download, tailor it to fit your specific needs.

PET ADDENDUM

It is hereby agreed by and between _____ (*Homeowner*) and _____ (*Guest*) that homeowner will allow guest to have the following described pet and no others in the vacation home upon and subject to the terms and conditions of the rental agreement and this addendum.

The permission granted herein shall be limited to a certain pet as described below:

Type of Pet: _____ Name: _____

Color: _____ Weight: _____

Age:_____ Sex: _____

Guest hereby agrees to comply the following:

1. Guest to pay additional pet fee in the amount of $_____ per (night/week).

2. All pets must comply with the following specifications (documentation from an accredited veterinarian must be provided by Guest upon request):

   a. May not exceed XX lbs.

b. Must be at least X year(s) of age or older.

c. Must be spayed or neutered.

d. Must be up-to-date on rabies vaccinations and all other vaccinations. Heartworm preventive is highly recommended.

3. All pets must be leashed at all times.

4. Guest is responsible for cleaning up any/all pet refuse.

5. Pets are not allowed on furniture at any time. Any evidence of pets on furniture may incur extra cleaning fees.

6. All pets are to be treated with a topical flea and tick repellent three (3) days prior to arrival. Fleas and ticks are very rampant in this area and can cause harmful/fatal illness to humans and pets.

7. Pet must not cause damage to premises or furnishings. If damages are caused, the cost of the damage may be deducted from security deposit or billed to credit card on file.

8. Guest should prevent pets from producing excessive noise at a level that disturbs neighbors.

9. Pet will not be left unattended for an undue length of time, either indoors or out. Pet will not be left unattended on balcony, patio, or porch. Pet must be properly crated if left alone.

10. Homeowner assumes no responsibility for illness or injury that may incur to pets or humans while on the premises.

The Guest shall be solely responsible for the pet while on the property.

Sign_____ Date_____

Housekeeping

Your housekeeping will have to spend extra time when cleaning after a pet has stayed in the home. The house must be cleaned assuming the next guest has a pet allergy. That means a close inspection of furniture, fabrics, and bedding for pet hair and accidents, a deep vacuum of all carpets, baseboards vacuumed, hardwood or tile floors vacuumed and mopped. The house must be thoroughly dusted as dander floats onto hard surfaces and lamp shades. Housekeeping will also need to check for any pet damage done to floors, fabrics, or furniture. Housekeeping should also note if there is any pet odor left on any fabrics, furniture, bedding, or rugs and report it to you immediately with a photo from their phone. Have a product on hand like odor-ban to eliminate any odor before the next guest arrives. Be sure you use a product that eliminates the odor, not merely covers it up, or the foul scent will return. There are many commercial products available but the above mentioned can be purchased as your local Sam's Club or Wal-Mart.

The time to clean after a pet has stayed costs a little extra but one night of your regular pet fee should cover the additional cleaning. Doing a deep clean after a pet stays also insures the not so routine areas of a clean get proper attention on a regular basis. Over all your property should maintain a higher degree of cleanliness because of pets frequenting and the extra detail required after their departure.

When baiting for pests housekeeping or maintenance must be very careful not to place toxic chemicals or bait where the pet can access and eat it. Although it is included in your pet addendum that you are not responsible for any pet injury or death, you still want to be prudent to prevent one from happening.

Pet Friendly Special Amenities

Have a dog biscuit for the pet waiting on top of your welcome letter to your guest upon check in. Wrap it in a bow- it just takes a minute and has a great effect. For singles and empty nesters this has as much impact as welcoming their child by name. Their dog is their family now.

Leave a leash on a hook by the door with a blinking walking light to clip on their dog's collar for dark areas. Have a flashlight on the hook for nighttime potty trips. Doggie waste bags on the hooks as well as a reminder that they are expected to clean up after their pet.

Dog water and food bowls are great to have on hand so your food serving bowls don't have to serve double duty.

Have a page designated in your Guest Information Book for those with pets. Include listings and directions to pet friendly restaurants, hiking trails, doggie day cares, groomers, and local emergency pet hospital.

Visit local independent pet stores and see if the merchant is willing to offer a discount to your guests. This will encourage guests to shop locally and provide them with a value.

Chapter 12
Decorating Your Vacation Rental for Guest Appeal

With Sandra Cloer

Covered in this chapter

- Simple Things You Can Do
- Things to Avoid
- When is it Time to Redo Your Décor?

Your home's décor is an area where your personal touch can have a huge impact on your VR business. With just a little more time, effort, thought and money, your home can go from being a place to stay to a destination in itself. Using a designer's eye and a coupon clippers budget, you can make your home stand out.

You know what the difference is between a blah house and a fabulous home. It's layers and layers of thoughtful, purposeful choices. Paint and floor coverings that infuse the home with warmth and style, furniture that will stand the test of time, curtains, pillows, and decorations that let you know that you're a valued guest in their home. Somehow, you get the feeling that they had *you* in mind when they chose the light fixtures, the rugs, and the gorgeous work of art hanging on the wall. After you take a tour of the house, you want to enjoy a glass of your favorite beverage and stay for a long time. It feels like home, only better.

If you create this feeling in your vacation rental, you'll have lots of bookings, happy customers, and five star reviews.

The décor you choose for your vacation rental and the furnishings you select show your respect and concern for your guests. If you throw some tired furniture into the house and have scuffed white walls, you're not going to get the quality of inquiries and bookings that someone who has put thought and attention into their homes gets.

Think ambiance. Think style. Think mood.

Hotels are cookie cutter. Room 323 looks identical to room 712. But you have the chance to shine, to make strangers feel like welcomed guests with your design style. Take advantage of this opportunity.

Simple Things You Can Do

Strive for beauty at every opportunity. Everything should be beautiful down to the Kleenex boxes and dishcloths. Have you ever been to someone's house who just gets it right? You know, everywhere you look there is something beautiful that catches your eye, yet it is not overdone. It makes you feel as if the person really took a lot of time to make their home welcoming and beautiful. That is what we want to create in our vacation houses for ourselves and our guests.

Pay attention to little details. Buy a beautiful soap dispenser instead of using the plastic ones that come at the grocery. Buy generic soap to fill them and they will soon pay for themselves. If you supply Kleenex to your guests make sure the box matches your décor or hide it in one of the beautiful boxes from a discount department store. Use a lovely container for your dish detergent instead of the plastic one it comes in. You will save money by refilling it with the off brand of soap. Don't buy the cheapest dish drainer, pick a nice one out that may cost a few dollars more but will look nice when left out. All of these little details matter. Everything should be as pleasing to the eye as you can make it.

Look at high end houses for inspiration. Maybe you believe you don't have a talent for decorating, but help is at your nearest bookstore or on the internet. Pick up a *Coastal Living* magazine if your home is by the shore, a *Country Living* magazine for a more rural area or *Pottery Barn* for something more classic contemporary. You can copy most anything in some fashion or another in an affordable manner.

Make a plan. When you shop look for great buys and clearance items. Never buy things without a plan for them just because the price is good. You may as well give your money away. Do buy things like coffee pots, toasters, pots and pans etc. when you find them for a great clearance price. Those are items you will need to replace at some point and it is easier and wiser to have them on hand. Keep a list on-hand of items you would like for your home in the future along with color samples to be sure your new treasures will compliment your existing décor.

Shop wisely. High end clearance stores like Ross, Marshals, TJ Maxx Home Stores, Burkes Outlet, Overstock.com , and Tuesday Morning have eye catching pieces that will stand out in your home. Watch your papers for sales at stores like Belk, JC Penny's, Kohl's, Sears, and Bed Bath and Beyond. Try to match sales with coupons for additional discounts.

Have a cohesive plan for decorating your home. Stick to three coordinating colors throughout your home. It is a simple way to give

108

your home warmth and flow. Choose no more than three coordinating fabrics in any room as well. You can change colors in bedrooms but don't go too dramatic. Keep things neutral so it will appeal to most people.

Theme or no theme? It is ok to go with a theme in your house but use it sparingly so it doesn't become a cartoon of the idea. French Country, Beach, Urban, or Retro are all nice, but don't go too zealous with any theme as you want your property to appeal to as many clients as possible. Less is more, unless you are trying to get away with just putting a couch and a coffee table in a room and leaving it at that. If you pick a theme, consider the location your home is in. Let's say it is in the mountains. You want to go with a "bear" theme. To make the theme work, only have three items per room with a bear on it. More than that and it can transcend into tacky.

Take a look at the competition. Do 90 percent of the VR's have a bear theme? Choose something that fits in with the mountain theme, but makes you stand out from the crowd, such as tasteful, local pottery or stunning photography or inexpensive antiques.

Use design in your favor. The opposite end of the continuum of theme is bare walls. Have you ever stayed at a vacation rental or hotel where your environment was white walls with a cheap framed picture? The last thing you want is your guests to feel restless and wanting to escape your home. If they want to spend their days sightseeing and their nights enjoying the town, fantastic. But they shouldn't feel chased out of your home. It doesn't take much to warm a place up. A few throw pillows on the couch, a rug, some nice silk plants and a few pictures do wonders. Don't take less is more to the extreme. Sometimes less is just less.

Go for the Ahhhhh. When your guests come into your home you want them to feel ...*Ahhhhh—I'm so glad I am here.* That translates into warmth and comfort. We spoke of paint, fabric, and theme and all of those will lend themselves to that feeling, but warmth is in the details. High quality silk plants are great for warmth. Soft lighting or up lighting can add drama to a room. Look for moments that capture your imagination without stealing the show. Use rugs and furniture placement to tie an area together or create separate spaces of use in a large room.

Make sure fabrics are comfortable and durable for guests. Look for patterns that won't show spills as much. Stay away from light colors or solids as they show everything. Leather is more costly up front, but worth the money in the end as it cleans up nicely and wears well.

Don't use your grandmother's furniture. Choose stylish pieces that will stand the test of time. Clean lines are best. You want enough on the walls to make it feel warm. Bare white walls feel very cold and sterile. Earth tones are great colors for keeping things warm and hiding blemishes on the walls. If you go with beach colors know they will need touch up more often. Use an egg shell paint that can be wiped down easily. Keep "magic eraser" in your cleaning kit as they really do work magic in removing scuffs from walls! Be careful though as they can be very dangerous to children if they rub their skin with it. It will cause severe burns.

Keep extra paint. Touch ups only take a minute, and can be done easily by mixing nine parts of paint with one part water. It takes an exact match to pull this off, though. So keep your paints in your owner's closet (not the garage, where the extreme temperatures can ruin it) and above all, keep the lid, where the exact recipe for remixing the paint is found. Label the containers so you know which room they go with.

Give people space both practically for their things, and emotionally to feel the space is theirs. Have you ever gone in some place and there was so much around you had no place to set your keys let alone your luggage? Less is more. You (or your housekeeper) are better able to keep up with missing or broken items if there is less to fuss with. Remember that your guests may have children, pets, or just be careless and things can and will get broken.

Expect normal wear and tear on things. Couches will get stained or torn eventually. Go for fabrics that will hide stain or better yet not accept it like leather. Dishes will get chipped and need to be replaced every couple of years. Forks will accidently be thrown in the garbage so it is good to have an extra matching set on hand.

Keep the items in your house in good order. If you let things become too run down guests are less likely to take care of what you have. It sends a nonverbal message that you don't really care. It doesn't mean that if something gets a small scratch that you need to replace it, just don't let it get to the point that it looks in disrepair. Of course, if you have an ultra-luxury home that rents for $5,000/night, you had better make sure things don't have scratches on them.

Things to Avoid

Making your guest feel like they are a visitor in someone else's house. If you have too many "personal" items around the guest may feel like they are intruding. Clear out all of your clothes, toiletries, and personal photos at the end of your stay. Put them in a locked closet to bring out again when you return. You may also want to have your own personal sheets and towels locked up. Your guests have paid for the home for the time of their rental, and they need to feel like it is theirs. It also generates a connection for them and they desire to return to "their" special place.

Some people advocate having family photos around. My philosophy is to do everything a hotel would do, then do it better.

Would you want to pay for a hotel room with Mr. Marriott staring at you from the walls and a collection of family photos on the table? If you do want to have one photo, place it in a general room, not a bedroom, and tie it into your locale.

I had a family photo in a grouping with photos of the locale, and the staff reported that many guests commented on how nice it was to see the family after having such a long e-mail communication. However, I changed the photos out for art, and no one has complained. If you have a family photo, keep it to only one. You don't want to remind people continually that this belongs to someone else. This is a business, and they are paying you for "ownership" for the time they are there, and that needs to be respected.

Putting irreplaceable items in your VR. If you can't bear to part with any particular item, don't put it in the house. You may have a particularly nice painting or your grandmother's china that you adore. Those are things to leave out of your property as they can be broken or stolen. Choose items that have no emotional attachment for family members in your VR.

Overlook Thrifting. You can find some great decorative items or pictures, or even big ticket items. Consignment stores, Craig's List, and Goodwill in high end areas are good places to look. Wealthy people give great stuff away.

Many people have found fabulous furniture pieces on Craig's List. Sometimes people are selling a house full of furniture that has been barely used or was only used to stage the house for selling.

Yard sales and moving sales are good places to hunt, too. People who are moving will sell things at a fantastic price just so they will not have to take it with them. You can purchase very nice washers, dryers, microwaves etc. from moving sales for pennies on the dollar.

Auctions after often overlooked, but you can find newer appliances and furniture.

You might question the used aspect of it all. As soon as someone stays in your house, everything will be used.

When is it time to redo your décor?

Sandra: *When is it time to take a look and update your décor? When you stop making bookings. Be careful, it is a slow fade and it just happened to me. I have one property that I just love, it was my first VR, and hadn't been updated since we opened. It was always one of my top booking houses. This spring I noticed great gaps in reservations. I went down to the property with a new eye, looking at it as if I were the guest coming in for the first time. Guess what? It looked used up.*

The path to the cottage needed a fresh bed of mulch and some of the large trees trimming. The porch furniture needed to be painted and fresh pillows added. A new rug was added and side tables for guests to set their drinks on. I went to Tuesday Morning and found some wonderful garden statues to set on the rail and lovely candles to set by the hot tub. I added succulents for life and green as they require little water or care.

Once inside, the wonderful dining table and chairs, that were quite expensive back in 1995 when purchased, looked like they were from, well, the '90s. I painted the chairs from green to black and put new covers on the seats. I took a pie safe and painted it black so it would stand out against the wood walls. I added a new braided rug under the dining room table.

I would have liked to replace the furniture but really couldn't afford to so I bought new pillows for them to give them a fresh face. Both beds got new bedding and I switched around some furniture and decorations from one room to another. I found some new décor items at a local thrift store. All in all the new look came to under $500.

I am pleased to say that with the new photos up online the cottage is renting again at a more regular pace!

Homework

Think of your three favorite homes to visit, or even resorts.

How did you feel when you were there? Stimulated? Relaxed? Pampered?

_____

_____

_____

What contributed to that feeling? Colors? Textures? Fabrics? Quality? Art?

_____

_____

_____

How can you emulate that in your home? List five specific things:

1._____
2._____
3._____

4._____

5._____

Professional Level Technique—check out the competition, including resorts. We just stayed at a state park, and there were only two choices for accommodations, and both were resorts. It was a great experience, as I found inspiration in every turn. Hotels are picking up on the home-like experience that vacation rentals offer, and are choosing textures and finishes found in upscale homes. Clearly, a designer had been at work.

All the more reason to up your game! Remember, you can get an expensive look for a bargain price if you are selective in what you spend your money on, and shop wisely.

Chapter 13
Organizing your Home for the Guest
With Sandra Cloer

Covered in this chapter

- Organizing Helps Guests Feel Comfortable
- Staging Your Home
- Lose the Clutter
- Kitchen Basics
- Bathroom Basics
- Supplies
- Living Room

Have you ever walked into a vacation rental and felt the last guests? Or maybe even the last twenty guests? Tattered magazines, mismatched coffee cups, and missing items made you want to ask, "Who's been sleeping in my bed?" Just like The Three Bears, things were off.

Professional Tip: The best vacation rental owners and housekeepers ensure that each guest feels like they are the first person to ever use the property. It's a worthy goal, and while things will happen, like a broken coffee pot your housekeeping finds two hours before check in, planning ahead will ensure your guests will be very happy. Since appliances break, forks get accidentally thrown away, and glasses shatter, keep extras in a place your housekeeper can get to easily. Your guests arriving in one hour will be none the wiser about the broken toaster housekeeping just found.

Guests notice trends. If they notice a note from the housekeeper stating the coffee pot was broken, but it will be replaced within an hour, and they find nothing else wrong, you won't have a problem.

But, if the coffee pot is missing, or put back with the broken handle in hopes that no one will notice, and the knife drawer is a safety hazard, and there aren't any trash cans in the bathrooms, and the light switches don't make any sense, and they can't find the broom, then, you have a problem. They will also notice things they might have passed on by, like a spider on your front porch, which many people might not be bothered by, but it's now part of their list against you. They pull the cushions out to look for the remote, which should have been visible on the coffee table, and find the couch littered with crumbs and a movie ticket stub from two months ago.

Organizing Helps Guests Feel Comfortable

By keeping things orderly and clean housekeeping is able to generate the feeling that your guests are the first visitors. It's an important step, as you are passing the baton from salesperson to housekeeping. You are still managing. But if you did a terrific job selling, and housekeeping doesn't share your vision, the guest will not be happy.

It is the little things that matter…

Like matching plates and glasses. If things are mismatched guests feel like you found all your kitchen supplies at the local thrift

117

shop. Matching glasses (even though inexpensive) allude to a higher end stay. Those little details make a difference.

A well equipped kitchen doesn't seem well appointed if you can't find anything. You also want to think of safety in your kitchen. Do not have a knife drawer with twenty different knives thrown in? Use a tray or knife block to keep them secure and edges down. Make sure you have a proper fire extinguisher in a readily accessible location.

Put like things with like things. All of your baking items, like mixing bowls, measuring cups and timers should be in one spot. It will make finding these items easier.

Have a container or designated drawer for cooking utensils. Again, they will be easy to find for the guest and it will be obvious where things should go back to when they are finished with them. It also makes it easier on housekeeping to check if items are all accounted for and clean.

Staging Your Home

Staging takes organizing to the highest level. The details, like arranging the coffee cups so all the handles are facing the same direction, making sure all cups are face up or face down (whichever you choose), all the dishcloths are folded the same way and in the same drawer, and making things look orderly lets your guests know that you care about the house and their experience. It is such a simple thing to do and often overlooked.

Lose the Clutter

Keep your things tidy, and guests will be more likely to, as well. People bring magazines on a trip, and then leave them behind. Don't let too many magazines pile up. It is nice to have a few on hand for guests to look through, but discard old or disheveled looking ones.

Don't let a pile of brochures from local attractions pile up. Place them in a notebook or basket for your guest to look through. Have a copy of the local, current tourist magazine available for them to find activities.

A good label maker is your friend. Use clear tape so it doesn't distract from your décor.

If there is a password for internet put a label on the router stating what it is as well as in the guest information book.

Have a laminated sheet with up-to-date TV channels.

Have directions of how to re-boot Wi-Fi, the cable box, or satellite box in case of power outage or other difficulty. If it is simple just label the box or router with those instructions as well as having them in your guest information book.

Put a label inside the fridge to remind guests to clean out remaining items at check out.

Put a label on trash can noting, "No loose trash in can, please."

Put a label on the back of the fireplace remote on how to work the gas logs.

The point is to make it as easy on your guest as possible. This will also prevent many after hour calls for a "how to" lesson.

Label light switches so guests will easily locate desired lights.

Label inside of cupboard doors with items located within is helpful for guests to put things away properly. This is also helpful for housekeeping to note if items are missing.

Kitchen Basics

- ☐ Good pot and pan set. Expect to have to replace every eighteen months or so.
- ☐ Dish set servicing twice as many as your property sleeps.
- ☐ Glass set servicing twice as many as your property sleeps.
- ☐ Wine glasses servicing twice as many as your property sleeps.
- ☐ Silverware servicing two to three times as many as your property sleeps. It is best to choose a common glass, plate, and silverware design that can be purchased again easily to match.
- ☐ Plastic cups
- ☐ Baking dishes
- ☐ Cookie sheet
- ☐ Pizza sheet
- ☐ Muffin tin
- ☐ Bread pan
- ☐ Cake pan
- ☐ Serving bowls
- ☐ Mixing bowls
- ☐ Pasta drainer
- ☐ Coffee maker (auto shut off and black is the best color to hide coffee stains)
- ☐ Coffee bean grinder
- ☐ Microwave
- ☐ Blender
- ☐ Toaster
- ☐ Hand mixer
- ☐ Crock pot
- ☐ Cutting knife set
- ☐ Steak knife set

- ☐ Kitchen scissors
- ☐ Pizza cutter
- ☐ Ice cream scoop
- ☐ Vegetable peeler
- ☐ Spatula
- ☐ Wooden spoon set
- ☐ Whisk
- ☐ Tongs
- ☐ Grilling tools
- ☐ Salad tongs
- ☐ Cake server
- ☐ Serving spoon set
- ☐ Knife sharpener
- ☐ Can opener
- ☐ Wine bottle opener
- ☐ Slotted cooking spoon
- ☐ Cooking spoon
- ☐ Flipping spatula
- ☐ Spaghetti spoon
- ☐ Potato masher
- ☐ Cooking fork
- ☐ Timer
- ☐ Salt and pepper shakers
- ☐ Paper towel holder
- ☐ Kitchen towels
- ☐ Kitchen dish cloths
- ☐ Pot holders
- ☐ Ice trays
- ☐ Tea pot
- ☐ Cutting board

- ☐ Measuring spoons
- ☐ Measuring cups
- ☐ Plastic pitcher
- ☐ Sugar and creamer set
- ☐ Vase for flowers
- ☐ Kitchen clock
- ☐ Trash can
- ☐ Dish drainer
- ☐ Place mats

Bathroom Basics

- ☐ Hair dryer
- ☐ Hand soap dispenser
- ☐ Two towels per person
- ☐ Two wash cloths per person
- ☐ Two hand towels per person
- ☐ Two bath rugs in each bathroom
- ☐ Trash can
- ☐ Shower curtain and liner
- ☐ Shower caddy
- ☐ Clock
- ☐ What you need in the bedrooms
- ☐ Trash can
- ☐ Extra blankets
- ☐ Extra pillows
- ☐ Extra mattress pad
- ☐ Reading lamp
- ☐ Clock radio (with iPod dock)

Supplies

- ☐ Dish soap
- ☐ Hand soap
- ☐ Laundry detergent
- ☐ Coffee filters
- ☐ Trash can liners
- ☐ Bleach clean up wipes
- ☐ Window cleaner
- ☐ Paper towels
- ☐ Toilet paper
- ☐ Scouring pads
- ☐ Flat stove top cleaner (if applicable)
- ☐ Clicker lighter
- ☐ Matches
- ☐ Bug spray
- ☐ Wasp spray
- ☐ Light bulbs
- ☐ Screw driver
- ☐ Hammer
- ☐ Measuring tape
- ☐ Pen & paper
- ☐ Manuals for grill, TV etc.
- ☐ Cleaning equipment supplies
- ☐ Vacuum on all floors
- ☐ Mop
- ☐ Broom
- ☐ Dust pan
- ☐ Feather duster
- ☐ Mop bucket

- ☐ Magic eraser pads
- ☐ Flash light
- ☐ First aid kit

Living Room

- ☐ Reading lamps
- ☐ TV (32" or larger preferred)
- ☐ DVD
- ☐ Radio w/iPod dock and CD player
- ☐ Container for magazines etc.
- ☐ Guest book
- ☐ Throw
- ☐ Adequate comfortable seating

Note- if you have a remote, budget or foreign destination VR, the above are suggestions to work from. Use your personal judgment with in these lists, and add to as needed.

It really is the little things that matter. Providing things that guests will need during their stay and having them easily accessible is a way for your guests to feel your concern for them. It's extending your customer service presence.

Homework

Go back and highlight or put a check mark next to items you need to get for your vacation rental. Are there any other items you need?

_____

_____

Chapter 14
Marketing—Web Real Estate and Beyond

Covered in this chapter

- The Web
- Overview of the Major Listing Portals
- What to Include with Your Listing
- Your Own Website
- Beyond the Web

Did you ever see yourself as CEO of a company? An entrepreneur? Because if you purchased a vacation home with plans to rent it out, you are now part of an exclusive club of business owners. Take a look in the mirror. What do you see? Think up a title for yourself— Owner, President, CEO, and welcome yourself to the club. It is work, but it's also a lot of fun. And it is time to get started on marketing.

Where to start?

When I first bought the land in Fiji and hired a builder, I didn't know the vacation rental market existed. I built in a neighborhood adjacent to a resort, and the resort owner who sold me the land agreed to book it out when they were fully occupied, about 25 percent of the time. He would make the majority of the money and I would get a small amount, but it would be something.

At the time, I had no idea how expensive things were—I was very naïve and went into it blindly. Utilities are outrageously expensive on an island. We have to have water, yes, "Fiji" water, trucked in during the eight months of the dry season. Electricity is a major expense. The staff budget necessary to keep things neat and tidy and guests happy is costly. There is no way this business model could have worked.

During the building phase, the resort was sold. To my utter surprise and grip of terror, the new owners didn't want to book my property. They planned on doubling the capacity of the resort and were busy with their own projects. I had just gotten back from my honeymoon, and we were plunged into fear—how on earth would I be able to market a property that takes twenty-four hours of travel time to get to from my home in North Carolina? We quickly put the not quite finished house on the market and I started researching dive magazines in Australia and New Zealand.

My makeshift marketing plan was that I could purchase classified advertising in the back of the magazines. I also started compiling a list of dive operators in the region that I could contact. But I made a critical discovery while doing my research.

I found that there is already a well-oiled machine for matching up vacation renters with vacation rentals. For the price of *two small classified ads in a print magazine, I was able to buy a year's worth of space on five different web portals. Full web pages with color photos, and lots of room for me to talk about my property.*

Now, here's the astonishing thing. When I bought listings in those first portals, I began getting lots of inquiries. And while the resort had promised me 25 percent occupancy with me just getting a cut, I was booking at 85 percent and getting all of the income. My first booking? The entire month of June. We quickly took the house off the market and have been renting by owner and making a profit ever since.

The Web

According to to a recent study by PhoCusWright, an overwhelming 82 percent of vacation rental travelers do all or part of their research online, and another 7 percent do a little research online. If you aren't marketing online, you are missing up to 89 percent of travelers. And the numbers grow each year.

So, what is your online position? Let's look at the web market together. The good news is that there are a few major players that are key to your success. They simply have too much of the market for you to ignore them.

The vacation rental market is dominated by large companies that act as high tech, spacious, photo rich, content filled brochures. They charge you a fee to get your listing visible to interested vacationers. While some smaller companies have a different business model, the large players do not charge a commission or charge you to see your inquiries. They make the same amount of money if you fill your calendar or if you don't make a single booking. It's simply a portal for you to connect with vacationers. The difference between a good listing and a poor quality one? What you, the owner, inputs. It's like a computer— garbage in, garbage out. Be thoughtful and purposeful in the photos you select and the copy you write. Don't over promise.

About five percent of visitors who click on a listing actually follow through and send an inquiry. People spend time dreaming and planning. You want them to inquire about *your* property. How do you do that? First, you need to get seen.

Since the vast majority of vacation renters look online for their next vacation, that's where you should start. Check out the major sites, FlipKey.com, HomeAway.com, VRBO.com, VacationRentals.com, and Holiday-Rentals.co.uk and see how many listings are in your area. Using Google, Yahoo, and Bing, search for "vacation rental _____" and insert your location. For example, Starfish Blue is listed via the major portals. In addition, I found that www.Travelmaxia.com and www.HolidayHomes.co.nz are good listing portals. A quick search on Google produced those results. Each area is slightly different in terms of what portals will be best.

Overview of the Major Listing Portals

FlipKey.com

A relatively new entrant into the vacation rental listing sites, FlipKey is majority-owned by TripAdvisor, a popular, free site where travelers report on their vacation experiences and help other travelers with questions. FlipKey focuses on reviews and photos.

The biggest benefit to FlipKey, other than the very fair price, is the relationship with TripAdvisor. All listings on FlipKey are automatically populated onto TripAdvisor, which has the largest online community of travelers, currently averaging 34,000,000 unique visitors each month. TripAdvisor attracts people at the beginning of the buy cycle. People who are considering a vacation and narrowing down their choices. The forums are well organized and peppered with questions like, "What's the weather like in Orlando in March?" or "Any family friendly places to eat on the Outer Banks?" On every page, there is a link to "Vacation Rentals" which takes you to a drop down menu where you put in your destination and your dates. FlipKey does the rest.

This one stop shop for research to reservation inquiries is the best utilization capturing potential customers in the full range of the buying cycle. Having VR's available in the largest online travel community, TripAdvisor, is a huge benefit to the VR industry. FlipKey's layout is easy to navigate and visually appealing.

FlipKey encourages owners to solicit reviews. You fill in the first and last names, e-mail, and date stayed, and FlipKey sends the review request on your behalf. The request is automatically accepted because you have verified them as a renter.

Reviews submitted on FlipKey for your vacation rental also show up on TripAdvisor. This is great exposure. Anyone can submit a review, but you can decline it if they didn't stay there. However, you can't read the review until you accept it. Should you get a negative review, you have an opportunity to respond. Read more on that in Chapter 27— Reviews.

FlipKey is an obvious choice for a newcomer and offers a huge value for your marketing dollars with exposure on both FlipKey and TripAdvisor and unlimited photos. It has produced quality inquiries for many owners, a high number of which turn into bookings.

HomeAway.com

In 2010, HomeAway brought the VR industry into the forefront of American culture by buying an ad on the Super Bowl. HomeAway hired

Chevy Chase and Beverly D'Angelo to reunite as the Griswalds, of *National Lampoons Vacation* fame, for a commercial and a fourteen-minute online video. The Griswalds' disastrous hotel experience culminates in a glorious vacation experience in a stunning vacation rental. During the 2011 Super Bowl commercial spot, they introduced the mod Ministry of DeTourism, again attacking the hotel industry, infamously with a flying baby doll that hits a wall. But whether you liked the commercials or not, they followed the marketing maxim, "Love me, hate me, just don't ignore me." Lots of people, including radio DJ's and newscasters, were talking about HomeAway in the days following both Super Bowls. HomeAways current marketing focus is a softer, "Let's Stay Together" that has a very appealing feel, showing the benefits of staying in a vacation rental.

Parent company of VRBO.com and many others, HomeAway has switched from a flat fee to levels, which currently range from $329-999. HA has the highest number of listings of any other portal. This can be good or bad, depending on the level of interest and competition in your area. They have recently added booking software as part of their offerings, and if you offer it, you will rank higher.

There is no charge except the credit card fee, which is on the low end of what's available to VR owners. It automatically updates your calendar, but if you don't use this service, or take a booking on your own, update your calendar as soon as you do, as this will help your ranking. Those who do not update their calendar often end up in the bottom of the heap. This is also good business sense by letting your guests know your current availability.

HomeAway went public in 2011, and now has a whole host of new owners—shareholders—that they are accountable to. They do spend quite a bit of money advertising, and are working hard to be synonymous with vacation rentals. "Let's HomeAway" is something you now hear.

131

VRBO.com

The first, true worldwide listing portal, VRBO has been around since the 1980s and was recently bought out by powerhouse HomeAway. VRBO, which stands for Vacation Rental By Owner, is a popular site with visitors and owners. It is now part of the HomeAway conglomerate and publically owned.

They also have a tiered system, and your rank is dependent on your tier and your tenure with VRBO. So, if you pay for the least expensive option, but have been with VRBO longer than anyone else in that tier, you will rank highest in the bottom tier. Someone who is brand new to VRBO but pays more for a higher ranking will be above you.

Vacationrentals.com

This number three site as of PhocusWright's study in 2010 is also owned by HomeAway, but doesn't carry the name recognition that VRBO and HomeAway have. It's less expensive and has less competition overall, and might be a good way to enter the market if VRBO is saturated in your area.

HolidayRentals.co.uk

If your locale has appeal to vacationers from Europe, HolidayRentals.co.uk is a great place to be. You can even pay extra to be listed on the French, German, Italian, and Spanish sites, including a computer generated translation. HolidayRentals.co.uk is also owned by HomeAway and can be added on to a listing on either site—no need to build a new listing.

What to include with your listing

Everything! You never know what will be your guest's top priority. A blender may not be your biggest feature, but if your guests may be dreaming of a frozen concoction on the deck each night, they might pass your property up for another one based on that small dream. Make sure you include every single amenity you have, from blenders to linens to hot tubs.

Some portals have items you can check off, like public pool or private pool, washer and dryer, internet, etc. Use the space where you can write narrative, or in paragraph form, to woo your guests.

Spend some time thinking about what you love about your VR and what your expected guest will enjoy. A one bedroom condo without a pullout couch will likely bring in couples. Even if you're in a city, you can set the scene for a full day of sightseeing, followed by relaxing with a glass of wine on your leather couch while a fire warms the room in the background.

If you have a six bedroom house—think about you're your renters will want. Likely, it will be families traveling together. What would Mom and Dad (the paying renters) want? Lots of activities so they aren't entertaining the crew constantly. PlayStations, pool tables, ping pong, a yard with toys, play this all up, but spell it out for them. "While your kids are enjoying the great outdoors in our fenced backyard, you can soak up the sun from our large deck."

Always keep the person who is paying for the holiday in the focus. A famous marketing quote, "sell the sizzle, not the steak." Make it exciting!

Create a mood. What is the sensation that people want to feel while they are vacationing? Is it an invigorating swoosh down the nearby slopes and relaxing in the hot tub at night, or a stimulating city visit, with an array of art galleries and cafes just outside the door? Talk about features as benefits to your guests. Paint a wonderful picture for them of your place in their minds.

Copywriting Hint: Understanding how search engines work is helpful in getting noticed. Search engines like Google and Yahoo love new content. They know their customers, the people searching, are hungry for new information. So, the search engines ignore duplicate copy, or writing.

To get the most bang for your buck, you need to rewrite your descriptions for each listing site and your own site. Don't feel that you can write copy once and forget it. Each portal you are on is like real estate on the internet.

Remember, you are writing for search engines, too. Search engines look at every page of information on the web. If you write one page and copy that from VRBO to HomeAway to HolidayRentals.co.uk to your own site, search engines ignore every repeat instance. So, instead of having four chances to show up on Google or Yahoo, you only have one.

Take the same information, the oceanfront balcony, the underground parking, the pool with plenty of lounge chairs, the proximity to the metro, and rewrite it. Then, when someone is searching for "vacation rental London" you quadruple your chances of being seen. In fact, copywriting for websites is such an important facet of having a successful website that an entire industry is built around SEO writing—which is Search Engine Optimization. The key, in a nutshell, is writing for people while including search terms that people interested in your business will find. More about that in Chapter 13.

Time saving tip: to get your business up and running, write one really great description, and copy and paste it into each new listing site. Once you have time, you can come back and re-write it to be fresh content for the search engines. The important thing is to get your property listed on three to five sites. Fast. Go back and tweak later on.

Your Own Website

Knowing that the vast majority of vacation renters use the web to search for their next vacation, you can see the importance of having your own website. They are too inexpensive and too common not to have them. And you are now the owner of a business—your vacation rental—that cost you a lot of money. If you bought a printing business for half a million dollars, wouldn't it be part of your marketing plan to invest in a website? If you are the owner of a restaurant, you would want a website with your menu, directions, hours of operations, and more online, wouldn't you? Treat your vacation home as a business. It is.

If you think it's too complicated to put up your own website, read Chapter 17. For many people, putting up their own website is a viable option. A warning. If you have a bad website, it will actually turn business away. Part of being a savvy entrepreneur is knowing what your strengths are and working within those strengths, and hiring out in your weak areas. Imagine walking into a pizza restaurant. They advertise wood fired pizza, your favorite kind. You can smell the aroma from outside, and you walk in, and can see the authentic wood pizza oven. Before you take your second step, you trip, running a bit to catch yourself on the counter. The owner looks up sheepishly, "I tried to tile it myself. Turns out, I'm not very good at it." Puts you off, doesn't it? You expect a company to hire out what they can't do well.

Free listings sites—The impulse is strong when you are first starting out to get your VR listed on as many sites as you can. Not all VR sites are created equal. Be very careful of sites that charge you to see an inquiry or charge a commission. The best sites spend money on advertising, bringing millions of visitors a year, some millions a month.

They do not get into the messy business of commissions and tarnish their reputations asking for payment for a lot of fishy sounding inquiries the month your listing is about to expire. That doesn't mean that every business which uses that model won't produce the level of inquiries you will need to convert into reservations, just do your homework. The sites listed in this chapter are well trusted and are real businesses, not scams.

Another reason to avoid the temptation to list on as many sites as you can is the time of upkeep. When you change your rates, or add a new amenity, instead of updating three to five sites, you could have twelve to twenty sites to update. Look for quality versus quantity.

Beyond the Web

If you aren't finding enough customers on the web, look at different places you can spread the word. Some overlooked places are:

Your competition—that's right, the VR next door could be a great source of inquiries and bookings. When a reservation comes in, but you are already booked, send them to your neighbor, and ask them to do the same for you.

Chamber of Commerce and Tourism Bureaus—Sandra gets a lot of last minute guests. She's on very friendly terms with her local Chamber of Commerce—even bringing them freshly baked cookies on occasion. They recommend her cottages to walk-in guests.

Local information sources—if your area is high in repeat guests, consider getting a listing on the local tourist map or other printed material.

Homework

Check out the big three—FlipKey, HomeAway, and VRBO and see what the competition looks like.

How many other listings on your area?

FlipKey   _____

HomeAway   _____

VRBO   _____

Do a search for your area and "vacation rentals." What other listing portals are popular for your area?

What is your marketing expense if you go with three listing portals?

_____

What is your marketing expense if you go with four listing portals?

_____

What is your marketing expense if you go with five listing portals?

_____

Note your three favorite listings and why?

1. _____
   _____
   _____

2. _____
   _____
   _____

3. _____
   _____
   _____

Chapter 15
Writing Engaging Web Copy

Covered in this chapter

- Inform and Invite
- Imagine Your Guests
- Beat out the Competition with a Welcoming Title
- Features and Benefits
- Finish Strong
- The Fun Part: Rewriting
- Editing Tips

Seven seconds to wow. That's really all you have at the most. When a person clicks on your page, you have seven seconds to let them know they are in the right place, and to give them a reason to stay.

Inform and Invite

Writing your listing or website copy should do two things; inform and invite. Readers should be able to get the basic information;

number of bedrooms, location, and type of house, but your writing should match the feeling they have when they are looking for a vacation rental.

The vacation rentals that receive the most bookings are not necessarily the best vacation rentals. They simply communicate what they have better than other owners, using stunning photos and imaginative copy.

The reader isn't looking for a two bedroom condo, even if that is what they end up paying for. The potential guest isn't looking for a five bedroom beachfront house, even though they may book it. They are looking for an experience. A feeling. A future memory. Something they can look back on when work gets stressful, the errands are endlessly boring, and the kids are crying. Evoke that place in their minds and hearts, and you will have a guest. Deliver on that promise, and you could have a calendar sprinkled with future reservations of lifelong guests.

Imagine your guests

Try to get a picture of them in your mind. They are actively searching for an escape from their life. You can see them, sitting in front of the computer screen, entering in search words on the keyboard. Write your copy thinking of them.

They are hopeful. *"Won't it be great to get away together?"*

They are happy. *"I can't wait!"*

They are full of expectations. *"A hot tub would be so relaxing!."*

Copy that is dull and laden with facts misses this anticipation. Also, copy that is too short misses the mark, as guests are eager to

139

imagine themselves in your property. A scrawny paragraph will send guests clicking away to the next listing.

Beat out the Competition with a Welcoming Title

Let's start with the title of your listing. If you are the reader, which one would entice you to click for more details?

Two bed, two bath condo with parking.

Beachfront condo with jetted tub in master suite. Beach chairs and views included.

These are actually the same condo. Both listing titles are truthful. But one is the clear winner by connecting with the guest. Which one can you picture yourself enjoying?

If you were going to toast your spouse at an anniversary party, you would go back to the time when you fell in love. When writing the listing paragraphs for your VR, go back to the time when you were making the decision to buy your home. It was the best of all of the ones you looked at for a reason. Why? And you can't put "It was the lowest price!" Surely, there were things that made you fall in love, so write these down here.

Why I bought my VR

Location

_____

_____

_____

_____

_____

Outdoors

_____

_____

_____

_____

_____

Kitchen

_____

_____

_____

_____

_____

Bedrooms

_____

_____

_____

_____

Bathrooms

_____

_____

_____

_____

Living Space

_____

_____

_____

_____

_____

Now, dig a little deeper. How do you feel when you are at your vacation home?

Here is a sample to get started.

I feel at peace and relaxed at Starfish Blue. In wonder of the beauty of creation. Like I've stepped into the most beautiful tropical painting. Stimulated by the coral reef in front of the house. Adventurous as I take a boat ride into new territory. In awe when I sit outside at night and sees the Milky Way, shooting starts, and meteors. Privileged. Like I've discovered a secret place. Magical.

What do you feel? Don't hold back.

_____
_____
_____
_____
_____
_____
_____
_____

Now, don't you think that there are a lot of vacationers who are looking for that exact feeling? Don't be shy in communicating the truth.

Features and Benefits

Features are facts. They don't necessarily mean anything to the guest until you show them why it's important. Turn your features into benefits. Benefits capture the heart and imagination, and you can get a leg up on the competition if you write in the language of imagination instead of facts.

142

A feature is a hot tub.

A benefit is spelling out what's in it for them.

"After a long day of seeing the sights of Los Angeles, relax in your private, rooftop hot tub with a glass of champagne and chocolate covered strawberries—which you can pre-order from our Amenity Packages."

Professional Level Technique: See how I painted a picture and then added an up sell? Hotels offer amenities, and if you live close by or have a trusted staff, you, too, could increase your income with adding amenities.

Here are other examples:

Feature: Deck and fireplace

Benefit: Smell the aroma of sizzling steaks on the grill from your treetop level deck. The leafy shade is a haven in the summer, dazzling in the fall, and inspiring in the spring. In Winter, enjoy the view from inside with a gas fireplace—just flip the switch and whoosh, instant romance.

Feature: Pool and view

Benefit: Lots of people dream about a pool. But the weather, the maintenance, or the expense keeps them from indulging in this luxury. Spend your holiday in a room just six steps from the blue tiled pool. Splash with the kids, or read a book from the underwater ledge, all while enjoying the view of three off-shore islands and the aquamarine to cobalt South Pacific on your front doorstep. Paradise awaits.

You probably have a good list now of positive aspects of your home. Now, just like a painter selects the right brush and just the right color, you have to put on a writer's hat just for about an hour, and think like a travel writer. Not easy for you?

Take some time and read travel brochures. Look to major companies who have hired top notch writers—major cruise lines and resorts are a great place for inspiration. Then, select your five favorite VR listings and read them with an eye for inspiration for your own listing. Of course, you are not looking for word for word sentences, but structure and style. Underline all of the active verbs. Then make a list of the verbs that you underlined in the travel brochures and VR listings. You should have plenty of inspiration.

Still feeling overwhelmed? As a writer, I have packages for VR owners. Contact me at www.VRFusion.com It's a tax write off and a onetime expense.

Your listing should be structured from big, sweeping descriptions that immediately let people know if they are in the right place, to more details, to a call to action.

Lead with the most important things first. Number of bedrooms are more important than the 600 thread count sheets. The big sweeping descriptions should be both informative and engaging. But there's another motive. It will help eliminate people who are not a good match for your property. If you have a one bedroom condo, those interested in bringing three families together over the holidays in one home will look elsewhere. It's time consuming to look for properties, so do what you can for the VR industry and offer clarity. However, honeymooners, retirees, young couples, and the solo traveler will be quite interested in your one bedroom condo.

Next, move in an orderly fashion to the smaller details. Start with your best feature—be it your backyard, kitchen, or number of well-decorated bedrooms, and paint them into the picture. Everything that is in the room or area that is a benefit to your guests should be described, using action verbs.

Read a book from our bookshelves from the privacy of the master suite on a cozy chair with ottoman.

Finish Strong

Finish strong with a call for action. What do you want people to do? Call you? Go to your website for more information? Give you their credit card number?

Invite them to do so.

We'd love to hear from you and help you plan your upcoming vacation. Call us today at xxx-xxx-xxxx.

For more details, visit our website at www.starfishblue.com for pages of information, photos, and videos. You'll also find an online reservation form and link for secure payment.

Make your reservation today to avoid disappointment. We sell out every summer.

Many listing portals have their own list of amenities—which benefits the traveler as much as you, as they get a quick picture of what you have to offer. So tick every box that applies to your home, then feel free to expound on those features in your narrative.

The fun part. Rewriting.

Each listing portal and your website should ideally have different copy. By writing four different versions of listings, you quadruple your chance of getting noticed by the search engines. This is especially impactful in areas with less competition.

When rewriting, you need to change a substantial amount of the wording for the search engines to read it as new information. It's not enough to change a word or two to get the benefit of this technique. Search Engines vary, but they usually need 300-400 words to see it as true content. They often will not scan something that is less than 200 words.

Keywords—make sure you use the town or area two times in the copy. Weave it in naturally, such as, "Just ten minutes by car from the heart of Ft. Lauderdale, our quiet neighborhood is a haven of relaxation after a fun day shopping." Further down the page, you would want to mention Ft. Lauderdale again, something like, "Ft. Lauderdale offers a wide variety of outdoor fun, from boat tours of homes of the rich and famous, deep sea fishing charters, and parasailing."

Editing tips

It's perfectly acceptable to write one stellar listing and plug that into all of your listings, lots of owners do that. But the really great marketers come back after everything else is running smoothly and rewrite the listings. You can put it on your "To Do" list, and rewrite one a week or a month.

Before you publish a listing, save it in a file, and put it away for a day. Then, read it again. You will likely catch things that you did not the day before.

Read it out loud.

Ask three people to read it, and give you their input. Sometimes, things are clear in your mind, but confusing to a reader. Encourage them to be honest with you.

Homework

Try your hand at writing the title. Include details and make it inviting.

Facts_____

_____

_____

Inviting Details to Weave In

_____

_____

_____

Now, write three versions of an opening paragraph, aim for four to seven short, evocative sentences.

Version 1

_____

_____

_____

_____

_____

_____

_____

Version 2

_____

_____

_____

_____

_____

_____

_____

Version 3

148

Chapter 16
Capture Your Home with Inviting Photos

Covered in This Chapter

- Snapshot or Work of Art?
- Tips for the Best Photographs
- Stage Your Photos
- Evoking Emotion

A picture is worth at least $10,000. Possibly even $100,000. Think about it, would you rent a vacation rental without photos? No, you would click right on to the next one. You can't expect anyone to plan a vacation, give you their credit card number or send you a check without giving them a clear picture of what they are purchasing. By producing high quality, emotion driven photos, you can beat out your competition, who will often just have informative photos.

Snapshot or work of art?

A photo can be a snapshot or it can be a work of art, evoking a feeling of longing. If you don't feel that you can take a photo worthy of your vacation rental, don't! Hire it out, barter it for a few nights, or exchange another service. Photographs don't have to be expensive, but they have to be great. Not OK, but great. Not good, fantastic.

What's the difference between a picture and a photograph?

Thought. You should plan your photos carefully. Start noticing the details. Consider everything. A good photograph will help you notice things you hadn't before.

I ordered some high end, leather furniture for Starfish Blue while I was still at home. It was thirty-four e-mails back and forth with the furniture company, and more with my manager, to choose the furniture, negotiate the price, set up delivery and finally, the placement. I could hardly wait to see the photos.

Our home was in between guests on delivery day, so there was no clutter. Or so I thought. My eye first scanned over the sumptuous furniture, then my eye screeched to a halt on the magnificent palm wood bar behind the sofa. A pink box of tissues and 2 royal blue flashlights arrested my attention and halted my enjoyment of the room.

I came up with a new policy—if it is going to be out, it needs to be beautiful. We have occasional power outages in Fiji, and we have spent a lot of money on a generator—and I need people to be able to find their way should the power go off at night. However, we didn't need two plastic flashlights displayed on one of the room's highlights.

The photograph was immensely helpful to me in determining what to do with the flashlights, tissues, and to establish the policy— only beautiful things should be visible.

A note: pictures should accurately display what they will see when they first walk in. My policy of only beautiful things should be visible wasn't just true for the photos, it is our policy from now on, all of the time. Don't be misleading in your photos.

Tips for the best photographs

Consider the light—morning or evening light is best when taking photographs. The light rays are low and long, leaving a warm glow. I was on a cruise recently, and the view from the balcony was of shipping containers—those big, metal boxes that are pulled by eighteen wheelers. Around 5 o'clock that evening, the whole area was aglow as the sun was going down. So much so that I grabbedmycamera and started taking photos—the clunky, industrial containers were transformed into a thing of beauty by the power of sunset light. Use it on the outside of your house or landscaping, and you'll have an evocative photo.

Indoor Lighting—a red flag to vacationers is photos of insufficiently lit room with dark corners. It makes people think of bugs and spiders and cobwebs.

Lamps are an inexpensive way to add value and further enhance your décor. Make sure you have enough lamps, and have them on for your photos. This will reassure guests that after a long day of touring they can enjoy an evening with a good book. You can take some artistic photographs of the light. If you have hardwood floors, look for the way the afternoon sun plays over the boards. Does the outdoor light make your décor light up? Take a photograph.

Angles—we often look at things from one way when taking photographs. Stand at one end of the room and *click*. Sandra and her husband hit on the art of thinking outside the box with the position of the camera. She and Dean got up on chairs and put the camera very near the wall for an artistic look at the wall art in one of her cottages.

My next trip to Fiji, I took the camera into the pool. The photos were amazing. The first part of the photograph was the silky blue water—who wouldn't want to be in there? Then your eye moved up to the palm trees towering above the water—that shot alone has swayed some people to reserve. It's more than reporting the facts, it's inviting the viewer to place themselves in the photo. To imagine themselves living out their dreams.

Photograph everything! Everything should be there for their inspection, from bedrooms, to bathrooms, to kitchen, living room, dining room, outdoor, surrounding area, garage, back porch, laundry room, to entry way.

Hotels are a known. If you book a Hilton, you have a general idea of what your experience will be like. Not so with vacation rentals. The more they can peek into your home, the more comfortable they will be.

Do not mislead with your photos—it's expected that the highlights be played up, but also show things that are realistic—your guests will thank you. At Starfish Blue, there are about thirty steps going down to the water. And we don't have much sand. I have photos of both on her website, www.starfishblue.com —a view going down the stairs and a view from the water, which clearly shows the house is not at water level, even though we are absolute ocean front. It's not fair to play with someone's vacation time and money.

152

If your house doesn't have enough good qualities to photograph well, either change it so that it does, or consider that it might not be a good vacation rental.

Remove the clutter—look at the room, then take the photo. If possible, take a lot of shots of your house, both inside and out, and immediately put it on a laptop or computer. Seeing it blown up on a monitor will help you know if there is something distracting—like the door to the laundry room with the load you are working on in between guests. You want to be truthful, but you also want to let the beauty show.

Time Saving Technique—most cameras have a very high resolution, which create pictures that are way too large for the web. Check with your web master, and ask what resolution you should take the photos. They may ask for two resolutions, one for thumbnails, and one for when the photo is clicked on and it expands. Then, take the photos in the resolution(s) that the web master requested. It will save time later on not having to resize them.

Take photos both ways—vertical and horizontal. Some shots lend themselves to one orientation or the other, so make sure you have a choice.

Take photos that leave room for writing—you may want to create an ad and use part of the photograph for words. Blue sky, flooring, and grass make for good areas to write text.

Take the many moods of your home—your home awash in bright morning sunshine is very different from a romantic tableaux, where you have a close up of the dinner table lit by candles.

Stage Your Photos

Your property should be well furnished for the needs of your guests. Plenty of kitchen chairs for the number of guests, seating in the living room, linens, towels, etc. However, for photos, you can use your imagination and go one step further. While you wouldn't have two glasses of wine sitting out and a fire in the fireplace when your guests arrive, if you have wine glasses and a working fireplace, it's conceivable that they will create that scene. So, get a bottle of wine, set it on the end table, light a fire, drape the blanket across one side of the couch, and play around with angles until you get one that will make them say, *"Ahh, wouldn't that be romantic."*

The only things I recommend to bring in for a photo shoot are flowers, luggage, and food. These are items that the guest would likely bring. Even so, I only recommend using flowers if you actually provide them, if not, there could be a slight disappointment when the guests arrive and the table looks less appealing. Make sure you have a variety of staged shots and photos of exactly what your VR will look like when they arrive.

Look around at your house. Where could you add inexpensive touches that create a mood? If you have a bathtub, could you get one of the trays that fits across it that will hold a book and a glass? If so, fill the tub with water and bubble bath, put the tray across the bath, and put one of your books from the bookshelf, add a pop of color on it, maybe a single flower in a silver cup. Then take the pictures while the bubbles are still high and inviting. Of course, you will leave the tray so that the guests can recreate that scene for their own enjoyment.

Evoking Emotion

Think of your favorite books and movies. What is it about them that you remember? It probably boils down to emotion. The fervent hope of a Jane Austin book, the edge of your seat fear in *Hunt for Red October*, the happy ending (in the last ninety seconds!) of *The Pursuit of*

Happyness. Your guests are unconsciously looking for that. They don't want to just see a room with a bed, although that's a good start. They want to see a turned down bed with two pillows on each side, a book, and chocolates and a poem on each pillow. In Fiji, we use flowers on the bed. Create a mood, and make sure the mood will be sustainable while they are there, and you have a winner.

Label your shots—if you are near a beach, but it isn't on your property, it's perfectly acceptable to include a shot of it, as long as it's properly labeled. Do not have it as your opening shot. Order your shots starting with overall, sweeping photos, such as the front of the house and the kitchen, to detail shots, then finish with photos of your area. When labeling an area photograph, include the name and the distance from your house. For example, "Delray Beach. A ten minute drive from our VR." or "Starbucks Coffee—a block from our condo." Guests will appreciate your honesty. No one wants to be misled by a photograph that isn't accurately portrayed.

Plan your shots—make sure you photograph everything, many times. Often, when you get home and load your photos on the computer—you'll find something out of place. If you take multiple angles of each area in your house, you should have plenty to work with.

Have a file with photos just for you—I am twenty-four hours from my home in Fiji. Having a photo to look at really helps jog the memory. Do the bedroom doors swing in or out? Is there an outlet behind that chair? Did you find the perfect drawer pulls and handles? How many cabinets or drawers have a one screw hole pull, and how many two screw handles will you need? A log of detailed photos of each aspect of each room and your entire property can be a huge help to the long distance owner. Even if you live nearby, it is helpful to have a photo catalogue of your VR, so when you have guests in, you don't have to bother them.

Take photos each season. You can update your listings very easily, and when people are booking their fall trips to see the leaves, or the spring trip, when flowers are blooming, you can show your vacation rental with what they are expecting. On other sites, where you can have unlimited photos, like FlipKey, you can have pictures of your VR each season all of the time.

Take photos often—good owners will be making small changes and big updates to their rentals throughout their ownership. If you restain the deck, put a photo up with the new color. If you add to the décor, and change paint colors and throw pillows in the living room, put a new photo up. You never know who's lurking. Some of my guests have been dreaming for years, and visit the web frequently to check up on their future holiday. They will notice when things look freshened up and it will strengthen their resolve to make the dream a reality.

Take a variety of shots—including details shots. While sweeping views of the entire room is a must, having artistic shots of details, such as art work and architectural features, set you apart as an owner who cares about the details. Close-up shots make people say, "Look at that vase! Lovely. I wonder what else is there?"

One last piece of advice…

Back up your photos. Back up your photos. Back up your photos.

Homework

Find ten examples of fantastic accommodation photos. Look at magazines and online. What draws you in? What are common themes in all of them? Good lighting, staging?

Start taking photos of all areas of your VR:

Indoors

Outdoors

Area shots

Chapter 17
Your Own Website

Covered in this Chapter

- DIY or Pay Someone?
- Choosing a Domain Name
- Design
- Competition
- Easy-Peasy Templates

Every vacation rental needs a presence on the web. Ideally, each vacation rental should have their own creative, engaging website.

Are you intimidated? Don't be, there's a whole industry there to help you—everything from one stop shops where you can purchase your domain name, choose a template, build your site as easily as you move within Word. It's a matter of uploading photos and writing inviting copy, and then, click, you publish it, all for a very fair price.

You can be rewarded with multiple bookings on the small investment you made.

DIY or Pay Someone?

If you're still intimidated, all or part of the process can be hired out. Don't think you need to do it yourself. If it overwhelms you, treat it like you would fixing a leaky faucet or changing light fixtures. Call someone who knows what they are doing and has the expertise to create a professional website. For the price of high thread count sheets, you can have a one page website. For a whole bedding set, you can have a multi-page site. And it won't get stains and have to be replaced!

Choosing a Domain Name

The first thing you want to do is choose a domain name. This seemingly easy task can actually be the hardest part of the process. The web has been around long enough that a lot of the good names are already taken. But not all! So sit down with a piece of paper and a pencil, (yes, we're going 1990s on you!) and write out the perfect name. Chances are, it's taken. So, if it is, what are some variations?

Can you put the name of your town in with it?

Add the words "vacation rental" or "VR?"

Add a few dashes?

Come up with twenty different variations. Now, go to www.namecheap.com and see what's available. They have a function that allows you to search multiple domain names at once. If you see one in your top twenty, grab it.

How to choose a name?

- I was snorkeling in Fiji the first time I ever saw a dinner plate sized, electric blue starfish. It was so startling! Years down the road, when the property was ready to rent, I went back to that memory to name the property. And Blue Starfish didn't sound quite right, so Starfish Blue became the name. www.starfishblue.com
- Sandy's husband came up with the name, Cranmore Cottages. Why? Because the first two cottages they purchased were on Cranmore Lane. Simple. www.cranmorecottages.com
- The vacation rental next door to Starfish Blue is called Bularangi. The owners have one vacation rental in Fiji and multiple ones where they live, in New Zealand. *Bula* is the Fijian word for Welcome, and *Rangi* is the Maori (local New Zealand) word for Heaven—so Bularangi is the combination of two different words in different languages that together mean "Welcome to Heaven." www.bularangi.com

With a little creativity, we all got website domains that are memorable and meaningful. Hopefully you will, too.

Design

Even if you hire out the design of your website, which is much more reasonable than you might think, having a sense of what works and what doesn't is very helpful. Here are some industry standards.

A well done website enables guests to imagine themselves in your vacation home. To feel the leather couch, smell the salt air, dive into the refreshing pool. In fact, most studies show that you have seven seconds to wow them, or *click*, they are moving on to the next one. As there is more competition on the web, that number is getting smaller and smaller. Having a great looking website is essential. If you can't do it yourself, pay someone. A poorly done website will turn people away.

Competition

Don't lull yourself into the illusion that you have the luxury of time, that a visitor will be so determined to see your site that they will weed through poorly written copy, a cumbersome layout and fuzzy photos. Your goal is to wow them. You are competing with tens, maybe hundreds or even thousands of vacation rental websites in your area alone. And competing with about a million worldwide. Not to mention cruises, hotels, B&B's, packages, and tours. If guests are not intrigued immediately, they are moving on to the next one. This is your first connection with the guest. Go all out.

The good news is that going all out doesn't have to mean a lot of money. It means attention to the details in web design, copy, and photos.

Three Key Ingredients

There are three key ingredients that every website needs to do well to make a visitor stay.

Easy to Navigate and Understand

Imagine yourself walking into a business and faced with a hallway with eight or nine doors, all closed, all unmarked. How long would you stay there? It would be frustrating, you'd quickly move to the next shop. The same is true for websites. They have to be easy to navigate. Invite your guests in. Lead them through the site. Give them a reason to stay. Your menu should go across the top or along the left side, either is fine.

A simple but attractive header, which is the banner that goes across the top and holds the name of your company, will make you look professional. It may or may not include a tag line. For my vacation rental, "Starfish Blue" is the name of the company, and the tag line is "*All that's missing is you.*" Simple, compelling, and involves the reader from the first second. Your tag line could be as simple as your location, *Nags Head, North Carolina.*

The first thing you need to do is let the visitor know they are in the right place. If they searched for "Asheville" and they ended up on your site, they need to know that they are on a vacation rental website. They may be looking for plumbers in Asheville. If so, they will very quickly back out and change their search. If they key in Asheville and are looking for accommodations, you want them to very quickly know what you are.

Maybe they are looking for a home for a family reunion with six bedrooms. But if a couple is looking for a weekend getaway, and you offer a one bedroom loft with free parking and are walking distance from downtown, they should be able to find this information quickly. If it suits their needs, and the site is well designed, they will likely continue to hang out on your site, and maybe fill out a request. Bingo! Connection with a qualified guest, who could soon become a potential client.

Lots of research has been done on eye mapping, or where people look on a website. Do they read line by line, scan all over, or do they go down the side? The research shows that they work in a triangle or F pattern. First, they quickly scan the top, then down the left side. If they like what they see in those two areas, they scan the area in between. However, as they go down the page, they increasingly stay to the left, following the lines of an F. Key information should be in that golden triangle—across the top, down the left side, or in the area in

161

between. Photos get more attention than words, so make your photos count.

Based on this information, menus now are increasingly showing up across the top. Not only is it in the area most likely to be seen, but it will always be seen by search engines and people, as it's "above the fold." Think of a newspaper. How often are headlines and stories that are "above the fold" read? I read them in the grocery store while I'm in line, but rarely do I move the paper to see what's beneath the fold; I have to be really intrigued. To get the rest of the website read, you have to capture their emotions with the information that is on their screen when they click on your link. Think of the part of your website that shows up on the screen without any scrolling as "above the fold."

Keep them on Your Site with Photos and Key information

It's all about the vacation experience, about your home and the surrounding area. You need to pull out all the stops writing compelling copy and using your best photos. Many owners use a slide show on the home page, like the one at www.StarfishBlue.com . Many people have said that they were captivated by that slide show. The movement is a bit mesmerizing. Paying someone to do a knock-out website can pay off quickly, giving you an advantage on the competition.

Then, start with a large photo, your very best one. One that evokes emotion. Go for the *Ahhh* feeling. Remember, you have seven seconds to captivate your audience. Create a sense of escapism in that small space. Key things that should be there are your company name, tag line, location, type of vacation rental, (condo, villa, cottage, lake side cabin) and how many bedrooms.

If your menu is across the top, on the left side, you can put your calendar or link to one, a contact us link, and other information that you want your guests to see. You could have a little icon with the current weather. Maybe a couple of quotes from recent guests in italics,

162

such as, *"Our best family vacation yet."* and *"Already looking forward to next year's vacation at your lovely home."* Links to Social Media are important and should go on the upper right corner- which is industry standard.

Menu- while one page is good, about 6 is much better. This really allows a person to spend time on your site, exploring and feeling comfortable that this is a solid, stable business as well as a comfortable home away from home. In keeping with current data, I recommend that the menu on a new site be across the top or on the left.

Colors—choose two primary and one accent color. A cabin would work well with warm, fall, earthy colors. A beach house might have a blue/green theme with yellow accents. Keep type a sans serif font (Verdana and Calibri are good options.)

Background color. Do not use a dark background with white type, with the possible exception of a title and photo gallery. Generally, people read about 40 percent slower with light writing on a dark background. It makes people go, *click*, and move to the next website. A trick of the trade is to use a very light background color (like a light cream) and a dark gray font. It appears black and white but it's easier on the eyes. But black type is very common and will not be a problem.

Easy Peasy Templates

We are in the third round of edits with the publisher, and had to stop and include this resource. www.WebChalet.com offers VR websites. This company is the answer to your design issues and expense. You can have a domain that is www.yourcompany.webchalet.com or have your own domain name that is www.yourname.com.

These easy to use templates offer easy uploading options, a one-click link to area restaurants and local attractions powered by Yelp, links to Social Media, and more. You can make your own page of recommendations for restaurants, or link to Yelp, and let travelers and locals sort out their favorites and not so very favorite. WebChalet gets Social Media and it's well worth listing with them and including their easy to use add-ons that will keep visitors on your site longer.

"While listing directories have played an important role for vacation rental owners to have an online presence, the next trend is for owners to capture leads with their own website. Linking all of your advertising efforts, including social marketing, back to your own website is a sustainable long-term strategy."

- Chad Brubaker, WebChalet, CEO

WebChalet has beautiful, beautiful stock photos as their default photos. As I always advocate, being utterly truthful in advertising is the only way to go. So use these stock photos as inspiration, and use your camera to take photos of your own property and your own town that evoke the same feeling of awe or quietude or energy, and recreate that. Take close up photos, wide angle photos, and detailed photos of what they will experience not only at your house but while on vacation, and label them clearly. If the lake is a mile away, mention that, and play up what they will see along the walk.

A line of premium, Beth Carson Designer templates are in the works. Check out www.webchalet.com for details.

Homework

what are your top five favorite travel websites? Why?

www._____.com

_____
_____
_____
_____

_____

What can you use as inspiration for your website?

_____

_____

_____

_____

www._____.com

_____

_____

_____

_____

_____

What can you use as inspiration in your website?

_____

_____

_____

_____

www._____.com

_____

_____

_____

_____

What can you use as inspiration in your website?

_____
_____
_____
_____

www._____.com

_____
_____
_____
_____
_____

What can you use as inspiration in your website?

_____
_____
_____
_____

www._____.com

_____
_____
_____
_____
_____

What can you use as inspiration in your website?

_____
_____
_____

_____

_____

How many pages do you plan to have in your website? _____

1. _____
2. _____
3. _____
4. _____
5. _____
6. _____
7. _____
8. _____
9. _____

If you already have a website, do you have any plans to make improvements? Update photos? Rework web copy?

_____

_____

_____

_____

Do you plan to hire out the work or do it yourself?

_____

Chapter 18
Social Media - The Basics

Covered in this chapter

- Why Social Media
- TripAdvisor
- Facebook
- YouTube

Entire books have been written on Social Media. To the uninitiated, it can seem overwhelming. As a vacation rental owner, you do not have to be an expert to get ahead of the competition. By incorporating a few tips, you will be harnessing the power of free social media in no time.

Why Social Media

Social media is in its infancy. Even with hundreds of millions of users worldwide, the potential is growing exponentially. New to Social media? Don't know the difference between a Tweet and a Like? A Friend and a Follower? The good news is you don't need to be an expert to get value out of your efforts. It's actually quite easy.

Which sites should you focus on? You can spend a lot of time spinning your wheels. From LinkedIn to Twitter, each site offers a different market twist. I recommend utilizing just three: TripAdvisor, Facebook and YouTube, all of which are free.

TripAdvisor

A listing on FlipKey also gets you listed on TripAdvisor, the world's leading site for travelers seeking information. TripAdvisor has tens of millions of unique visitors a month, and it's traveler sharing information with other travelers, writing fresh, organic content. Travelers even have the ability to upload photos of their travel experiences online. More and more, people are seeking the advice of real travelers over marketing material. As a bonus to FlipKey owners, guest reviews show up on TripAdvisor, which is a huge value add.

TripAdvisor also has a menu button for Vacation Rentals on every page, so any of the tens of millions of people searching TripAdvisor each month will have access to your vacation rental.

But don't stop there. People go on TripAdvisor when they are planning any kind of a trip. Feed the interest of potential vacationers to your area. While TripAdvisor has strict rules against promoting your own property, pay it forward by recommending restaurants and activities, and answering questions related to weather and things to do. Have your goal be promoting your region, not your home, and you'll contribute powerfully to this online community. Other hospitality owners and travelers will take notice and appreciate your input.

Note- if you are trying to build a brand on TripAdvisor as a helpful source of information for your area, remember what your mother said. If you can't say something nice, don't say anything at all. If it's on the internet, it will likely be up there forever. Consider yourself a promoter of the industry and keep quiet about the negatives, especially in your competition. Never, never, never say anything bad about your competition. If it is truly bad, word will get out, and it's best that it not come from you.

Facebook

Facebook is relationship building. It's free, easy to do and does not have to be a drain on your time. Some businesses need a huge Facebook presence. If you are the owner of one or two vacation rentals, you should be able to have a Facebook presence in as little as 10 minutes a week.

First, you need a personal page to get online with Facebook, then you can add business page. Upload some great photos. Add a few posts. Once you are up and running, invite your friends and past guests to be fans of your page. I post a Picture or Video of the Week once a week to the Starfish Blue Facebook page. If business were slow, I would be more active. Join us at http://www.facebook.com/starfishbluefiji .

Think about what your guests would want to see and deliver. No one wants to hear a constant barrage of not so cleverly disguised sales pitches. It comes across as "Pick me, Pick me." But if a new sail boat operator opens up or there is going to be an art festival in your town, these are things that will interest your guests and future guests.

Ideas for posts to your Facebook Business Page

- Upcoming tourist events
- Pictures

- Invite your guests to share pictures
- Discounts for last minute or hard to sell weeks
- Comments from exceptionally happy guests
- Invite your guests to share their experiences
- Discounted airfare to your destination or other travel bargain
- Positive, newsworthy items about your city or local travel supplier
- Great experience you had enjoying your region
- New amenities or features

Like, Like, Like- Facebook is a circle of positive actions. Like your favorite local Italian restaurant, dive shop, friends and airlines. In return, most people will do the same for you. You'll grow and grow and grow. The more Friends you have, the more access you have to their friends. Spend some time seeking out other tourist spots in your area and Like their businesses. Make positive comments on their wall.

Responding to comments is polite and expected. If you have a particularly active page and a lot of comments, it is perfectly acceptable to respond to multiple comments at one time. An example would be, "Amy, thank you for the great review on TripAdvisor! Paul, yes, we are directly on the beach. The sound of the waves is utterly relaxing."

YouTube

YouTube is no longer just the playground of teenagers showing off their skateboarding stunts. As of 2012, it is the number 2 search engine in the world. Google than YouTube.

Pretty powerful.

It has a huge professional population as well as a large teen following and everything in between. If you want to research the Prius, learn how to tie a sailboat knot, or find out the best rides at Disneyland, then YouTube offers a lot of information in the form of videos.

If you want a free commercial, YouTube is the place to do it. You do not need a fancy camcorder or special software, a cell phone can work. Videos are easy to take if you follow a few simple rules.

- Keep the camera steady.
- Pan slowly. Don't give people motion sickness.
- Keep each clip of your video at least ten seconds long.
- Connect separate shots rather than walking through your house or yard.
- Avoid multiple zoom in and zoom outs. Adjust the zoom slowly.
- Stage your rooms.
- If interviewing people, check the sound quality. A windy day can muffle voices.
- As with photos, consider the light. Morning and late afternoon are good times to film.

If you don't have video of your property, you can download free photo software from www.picasa.com and string photos together. On Picasa, simply select the photos, then you can add text, ending with your website address. Once you upload it to YouTube, you can add music, but beware, sometimes the free music selections come with ads of your competition.

Make sure you utilize all of the keyword tools available. YouTube offers robust marketing and allows you to place a description and keywords, so someone searching for your area might come across your video. A few tweaks of the keywords for the Starfish Blue video took it from page five to page one of Fiji Vacation Rental.

Think of what search terms your potential guests would look under. A recent search for "Kiawah Vacation Rental" only brought back forty videos. Are there only forty videos of VR's in Kiawah, or only forty social media savy owners that put in keywords that described their Kiawah vacation rental so that searchers could find it?

Consider doing a variety of videos, including one that focuses on just your vacation rental, then do one that focuses on the surrounding area. You can get creative and do "10 Things to Do in Sitka," "10 Fun Places to Eat in Boston," "Secrets to the Florida Keys," whatever you feel like. Travelers searching for Sitka, Boston, and the Florida Keys will find your video and your VR as a result. And at the end, put a plug for your vacation home with your web site or phone number. The longer you can get people to spend time in being wowed by your place, the more likely they will be to contact you.

The goal of using social media is for you to become the go-to place for the client to find information to help plan their vacation. It also gives you a platform to be able to quickly let past and potential guests know about vacancies and specials.

Feeding them interesting content and helpful information is the key. WebChalet.com, a company who offers VR templates, provides seamless integration with social media. Consider adding Yelp, which is a popular site for restaurants and activities, as a no hassle addition to your site. This is a "set it and forget it" link, giving your guests easy to find content on your area, all written by other people.

And last but not least, Pinterest.

Pinterest- A popular social media spot with brides-to-be (is your place good for honeymooners?) and anyone who likes to travel is Pinterest. People can spend hours pinning their favorite photos of decorating, art, shopping, travel and more. And since each photo points back to the website it was "pinned" from, it's a great way to bring visitors to your site, especially if you have a particularly stunning house or view.

This site makes a lot of sense if you are already on Pinterest. You can also put Pinterest buttons on your site, so that people can easily pin your photos to their boards without ever joining Pinterest.

Homework

Join the conversation on TripAdvisor at least once a week. If you are not a member, sign in with your Facebook account and connect the two. Select the town your VR is in, and spend a few minutes a week answering general questions.

Open a Facebook account if you don't already have one. Once you have a personal one, you can create a Page for your VR.

Plan out a video highlighting your vacation rental. Use Picasa to string together photos and upload via YouTube, or put videos on YouTube. Make sure to enter description and keywords.

Chapter 19
Converting Inquiries into Sales

With Sandra Cloer

Covered in This Chapter

- Inquiries—Happy Occasions
- Closing the Sale
- Understanding Your Guests
- Ways to Answer Quickly
- Email Responses—Professionalism Pointers
- Signs of an Amateur—Things **NOT TO DO!!**
- Sample E-mail Responses

Getting clients. It is all about getting heads in beds, isn't it? You can have a perfect home, terrific listings, a knock out website, but it you fail in sales, you will still have low occupancy. The good news is that by following a few simple steps, you can beat your competition and fill your calendar.

Inquiries—Happy Occasions

Let's begin with shifting our paradigm and begin to consider inquires as happy occasions, instead of an interruption to your busy schedule. We are fortunate in our vacation rental industry as potential guests contact us with interest; we never have to make a cold call to solicit business. All of your work in selecting listing portals, taking fabulous, properly staged photos, writing inviting web copy and having a website have paid off. Success!

Your perspective guests are in the midst of planning a vacation, choosing where they will spend their hard earned money and limited vacation time; they are looking to you for answers and likely some guidance. They have taken a chance on the vacation rental industry, you in particular. You have an obligation to answer their request promptly, thoroughly, and courteously.

Closing the Sale

The key to having success in your VR business lies within your ability to close the sale from these precious inquiries. It isn't as daunting a task as it may seem, it simply requires listening to your guest to gather information about what they are seeking for their stay, answering all their questions thoroughly and completely without exaggerating what your property has to offer, and quick response time to their inquiry.

Understanding Your Guests

Try to visualize behind the scenes of a prior conversation a husband and wife may have had before they even began their hunt for a location to stay. The conversation possibly went something like this.

Wife: *You know what Honey, I would love some time to just get away with you.*

Husband: *Yeah. It's been tough at work lately.*

Wife: *I know, I feel like I hardly see you anymore. Where would you like to go?*

Husband: *Someplace quiet.*

Wife: *I was hoping for a little shopping, maybe take in a gallery.*

Husband: *Can we afford it?*

Wife: *I am sure if I look hard enough I can find something we can work with. We really need a break. Let me just look to see what is out there.*

Husband: *Ok, take a look. Let me know what you can find. If it is affordable I am in.*

Of course you don't hear any of that, all you will get in your inquiry is "Is your property available for the dates of May 6-8? What is the best rate you can give me? How close are you to the outlet mall? Party of two."

You don't have the backstory to fill in the blank spots to know they are exhausted, financially strapped, looking for someplace to be quiet and reconnect. Your detective work begins now.

You can answer the e-mail with, "Yes, it is available. The rate is $300 plus a $75 cleaning fee and tax."

Or you can reply more like this, "Thank you for your interest in our property, I would be pleased to have the opportunity to serve you and your companion as my guest! May is a beautiful time of year to visit.

At present, the condo is still available for the dates you have requested. The total cost for your stay would be $395.00; that is $300 for the condo, $75 cleaning fee and state & room tax combined of

$20.00. You can reserve on line at www.rentmyfabulouscondo.com or with me directly at 555 555-5555, which ever your preference.

If you don't mind sharing with me the occasion for your visit I can better help you plan your stay. If you need any further assistance please do not hesitate to contact me as it is always my pleasure to help any way I can."

If you are fortunate enough to have your inquiry by phone the conversation might look like this.

You: (Be sure to speak with a smile on your face.) *Yes, the condo is still available. May is such a lovely time to visit, you will not be disappointed! Is this a special occasion for you?*

Potential guest: *"No, just need to get away for a few days, but my husband is worried about the cost.*

You: *"I can understand that. Tell me a little bit about the things you all like to do."*

Guest: *"Well my husband likes to sit and read and I like to get out and see a few things, like galleries."*

You : *"This sounds like the perfect spot for you then. I have chaise lounges on the balcony with an additional table and chairs. That is the perfect spot for reading and looking at the sea. We are also having a local artist fair on Main Street the weekend you are considering; I bet you would enjoy that. Would you like me to send you the link?"*

Guest: *"This sounds perfect! Yes, please send me the link."*

You: *"Your cost is going to be $395 total. That includes your cleaning fee and taxes. I understand the cost issue though, I would be happy to give you a $25 discount if you can reserve now. Can you tell me whose name you would like to secure your reservation with?"*

Guest: *"Really! Thank you! Oh, you can just put it in my name...."*

Do you see the benefit of taking a little time with your perspective guest to get the backstory of their stay? Because of listening to what she was looking for in her time away with her husband, you are able to speak exactly to what your property and local area offered to meet her specific needs. Knowing that price is important, you can offer a discount to sweeten the pot. You should have the room for a discount already built into your rates.

Beth: *I sent inquiries to three vacation rentals in St. Augustine. We only needed two nights, and it was for the same week. I checked the calendars of all three places, they suited our needs and were in our price range, so I asked what their best price was. One answered back with information, one never responded, and one responded like this*

"270 19 65"

I forwarded it on to Sandra, who read it from her phone, and wrote back, "You forwarded me an empty e-mail." It was so lacking in any detail that she read it as empty. How would you feel if you received this answer? The impression it left was that the homeowner was either cold and distant, irritated with the inquiry, or technically incompetent, too hurried to write a few short sentences. It did not leave the impression that he would be a helpful owner if something should go wrong. He had a 33 percent chance of getting the sale, fairly high, and lost out due to poor sales skills. His condo looked very nice, and had what we were looking for, but he didn't deliver as a salesperson.

Dollar Signs—Sandra's properties have over 70 percent occupancy year-round, compared to the 30 percent that area property management companies bring in. Starfish Blue has been at 85 percent, in an area where hotels average less than 50 percent occupancy. Stellar customer service brings in thousands of additional dollars. Bottom Line? For Sandra, it's $17,500 more than a property management company would provide, and that's before you deduct the 30 percent or more commission they charge. This amount is *per property*. Can you afford to lose customers? Read on to watch the dollar signs rise.

Don't make the mistake that your property is so fabulous that it is the only one they are considering. Often, people send requests to multiple properties. Answer fast, establishing a relationship with the potential guests before the competition does. Who is your competition? Not just the people in the same condo building or neighborhood. Or the same town. Your competition is the entire planet.

Ways to answer quickly

Choose an e-mail that is just for your business. It's more professional. You can get one linked to your website or a Gmail or other free account. Be aware that some providers automatically put e-mails from certain providers in the junk or spam folder.

Get a phone that has internet and have your e-mails automatically sent to your phone, with a happy sound (Sandra's is a soothing gong) to let you know it's a business e-mail.

Commit to answering 90 percent of your inquiries within three hours of receiving them. This is not when you get around to checking it, this is when it actually shows up in your inbox.

Happy Homeowner Tip—have an emergency line that comes to bed with you—in case of gas or water leak, guests getting locked out, etc. But I advise that you leave your inquiries overnight. Downtime is vital. Between the internet and Skype, you could have someone in Australia or Italy phoning with a general inquiry and they will feel terrible if they wake you up. Check your e-mail before you go to bed and again when you wake up, and give yourself a good night's sleep. Avoiding burnout is a good way to give great customer service. Set appropriate boundaries that work for you, and work within them.

Consider what goes into your inquiry from the customer's point of view. They are planning part of a much anticipated vacation that will cost them time and money. It will be a hassle, either a car ride or plane or train; they are entering the unknown. They have had numerous talks about it, narrowing down their choices from broad—city, mountain, beach, to narrow, your area, your town, your home. A lot of time has been put into this moment of contact, either by the phone or by e-mail. How you handle this initial inquiry of both details and hopes is vital to making the most bookings you can at the highest price you can.

The best of the best greet each phone call and e-mail inquiry by matching the guest's level of hope and dreams and expectation, no matter what you were in the middle of when they contacted you.

This seems obvious, but it needs to be said. The response rate in the industry is appalling. While I don't have statistics on it, most likely more than half of inquiries sent out are completely ignored by owners. I once had to send out thirty inquiries to get three responses— and this after checking ALL of their calendars and finding availability on all of them. That's a dismal 10 percent rate for hours of research.

Since you have invested your time and money into reading this book, I assume you are in the top 10 percent of owners who will answer e-mails. It is common courtesy that if someone asks you a question you answer it.

E-mail Responses—Professional Pointers

- Start by thanking them for inquiring
- Recognize their trip—"Congratulations on your upcoming wedding! Starfish Blue is a lovely place to spend your honeymoon."
- Detailed breakdown of price AND total price, clearly defined
- If you are already booked, offer an alternative, either another property or alternative dates
- Offer to make the reservation
- Be clear and concise when replying to them. Don't take three sentences to say what can be said in one.

Signs of an Amateur—Things NOT TO DO!!

Never reply in ALL CAPS.
Never underline.
Never change the font color.
All of these communicate to the guest they are too stupid to read what you have written. Use less verbiage so as not to clutter up the important points.

Real World Pointer from Beth: *Sometimes, I get an inquiry with ten or more questions. Fiji is a foreign destination for many people and they have a lot of questions. What I do is write a warm note in the beginning of my reply, then tell them I am going to answer their questions in the body of the email in italics. Italics are a more gentle, warm way of differentiating between their words and yours. I also break them up into different lines, each new question gets its own line. This helps me, because I don't have to go back and forth making sure I answer each question, and the guests have it all in black and white, personally answered.*

Sample E-mail Responses

You don't have time? You're already booked? Have a document where you store prewritten responses. Here are two samples, feel free to copy and paste or simply use them as inspiration.

Occupied response

Thank you for inquiring about _____. Unfortunately, we already have a reservation for the time you inquired about. Do you have any flexibility with your dates? You can visit our website and check our calendar at www._____.com If it doesn't work out this trip, we look forward to your visit on a future trip.

If you would like recommendations on other places to stay in the area, let me know.

Kind Regards,

Beth Carson

Thank you for inquiring about _____. We are delighted to offer you exclusive use of our vacation rental for _____, 20__ to _____, 20__. The rate for __ nights for __ adults and __ children is USD$_____.

You'll find this home a perfect getaway from the world—we provide

_____

_____

_____ (fully equipped kitchen, linens, towels, snorkel gear, a hot tub) and have an array of amenity packages to choose from, including wine and cheese or champagne and roses upon arrival,) visit our amenities page at www._____. com for more information. We are nearby _____(museums, waterfalls, shopping, towns, parks). Many people love to _____ (hike, shop, antique, swim, snorkel).

All you have to do is write it once and then customize it for each individual inquiry. If they ask questions, such as how far to the nearest grocery store, make sure to answer that question. It shows your attention to detail. If it's on your website, don't simply tell them it's on your website, they will feel belittled. Answer the question, and then point them to your Q&A page for more information. Understand, they might be looking at ten to fifteen properties, they can't be expected to remember details on them all.

Why do we recommend putting in dates and number of people? It shows that you read their inquiry and have worked up a specific quote for them. If you have it wrong, it's an immediate red flag.

Beth: *I have many international inquiries. Many countries write the day first then the month. I was using a new listing agency, and didn't realize that they used that format. The woman was inquiring about September, but I read it as June. In my correspondence, I told her we were full for those dates in June. She wrote back politely asking why I gave her dates for June, as my calendar showed availability for September. I immediately wrote back and corrected my mistake, and she was able to make a reservation, and I had a booking. Without confirming the details, I would have simply told them I was occupied. I always write the month out, to avoid the minefield of a major misunderstanding.*

Just as you've put together a canned response for e-mail inquiries, mentally put together one for phone calls. Answer the phone in the same way each time. "Cranmore Cottages, this is Sandra, how can I help you?" is how Sandra answers.

But before she pushes the button and puts it to her ear, she smiles. While they can't see it on the other end, they can hear it in her voice. It matches their eagerness and enthusiasm. Her smile infuses her voice with joy, creating a warm and professional experience from the first point of contact.

Notes from Sandra: *Never treat your calls as a nuisance. Guests can hear it in your voice if you are annoyed to take their call. Remember you are a business and your phone and e-mail are your link to your client. They WANT to talk to you or they wouldn't have called. Be sure to think of their perspective while chatting with them. They are excited about their trip. If they aren't excited it is your job to make them feel that way. Smile with every word you say, a guest will hear it in your voice.*

Are you naturally friendly? If not, you have to be excellent at turning it "on," or possibly admit that this is not the best business for you to run yourself. The majority of clients are reasonable, eager, and happy and want to hear that from you. Occasionally, you'll find a person who probably shouldn't be traveling. Since we only see them for a short time, it's possible they have just had a trauma in their life—a heartbreak, bad news, or other. It's also possible that they are just difficult people. More on them in Chapter 25 The Cranky Guest.

You should answer e-mails and phone calls with natural friendliness and an eagerness. If you are not met with the same, it's your first red flag. If the conversation takes a turn that makes you apprehensive, it's very possible that things can go downhill from here. If the prospective client starts making demands, or asks for things which you know are not a good fit for your property, it's perfectly fine to say, "I'm not sure that our property is a good fit for what you are looking for. May I recommend_____ property? I think you'll be much happier there."

Starfish Blue is on the coast in Fiji, right on a reef, and the best thing about it is the view, the snorkeling, the hanging bed, and the people. It's definitely a relaxation concept place—perfect for honeymooners, families wanting to reconnect, and anyone wanting to unplug from the world. It is decidedly limited in nightlife. If anyone mentions nightclubs, shopping, or fine dining, it's a waving red flag that they might not be happy there. I have a few properties that I'm comfortable recommending and point them there.

Good customer service avoids problems before they come up. And sometimes that means turning away people who will be unhappy with the experience you offer with your vacation rental.

No property meets everyone's needs. Sandra currently owns thirteen properties and manages three others. She spends time getting to understand the expectations of the person before recommending a property. She's had honeymooners inquire about a three bedroom, but then suggested a cozier cottage—a better fit for them.

One time, Sandra had a call from a woman looking for a getaway for herself and her sister. She was calling to reserve a 1920s refurbished property high on charm and period details—most people love it. She absolutely had to have two bathrooms. However, as Sandra talked to her further, it turned out that her sister was a bit of a princess who loved to spend time in the bathroom until she achieved the perfect look.

186

Red flag! Her sister was not going to enjoy a 1920s period house. Sandy turned them instead to a property that she manages but does not own, a newly built home that doesn't have any quirks. She lost a booking for her own property, but still kept the commission, and in turn, had happy guests.

There can be benefits from bookings you lose. A few years ago, building started on the empty lot next to Starfish Blue. Sure enough, the house became a vacation rental. I was able to turn so much business that Starfish Blue could not accommodate to the new owner that they offered me a commission. Instead of taking it, I decided to keep the relationship friendly, and as a result, a few years later, we get the occasional referral from the neighbor. The relationship has been helpful to both. Of course, if you are offered a commission, by all means, take it if you want, but there's a benefit to having a great working relationship with your neighbors.

Here's a hard truth. Managing a vacation rental is not for everyone. You are dealing with people who have high hopes.

Be careful of making a referral to another place you do not know well. If client has a bad experience you can be associated with it. Refer to quality VR's.

Keep a record of where you book from and where you are just receiving inquiries. So you can tell where your money is being best spent for advertisement.

Homework

Write two responses, one for when you're available, one for when you are booked for all or part of their stay.

Checklist

- ☐ Thank you
- ☐ Personal Recognition
- ☐ Price—breakdown and total—if international, make sure to include the currency
- ☐ Answer all questions
- ☐ If booked, offer an alternative.
- ☐ Offer to reserve
- ☐ Reminder of why your home is special—right for their needs.

Answer these two inquiries, one each for available and reserved.

Name: Kesha Smith
Dates: 9/2/2012
Number of nights: 7
Number of adults: 2
Number of children: 0
Additional comments: Hi, I'm looking for a place for my honeymoon. Is your place available? If so, how much is it? Do you offer any discounts for a week's stay? How close are you to the nearest grocery store? The nearest ABC store (liquor store)?

Response

_____

_____

_____

_____

_____

_____

_____

Name: Daniel Jones
Dates: 12/26/2012
Number of nights: 5
Number of adults: 2
Number of children: 4
Additional comments: Do you have blow up air mattresses?

OK—the second one was to get you thinking. What did you notice about it? Look at the date—it's the day after Christmas. If you already have a booking for Christmas, and they have decided on their own to leave the next day, then it's perfect. If not, you're going to have to find a guest that is willing to pack up everything the morning after Christmas and vacate, and make sure you can get housekeeping in there—you will want to make a clearly defined Holiday's policy.

Some people have a week minimum stay over holidays, some have three nights. If yours is a destination many people drive to, it might be a good fit, and five nights would be better than your three night minimum. If most of your guests fly in, you might want to have a week minimum over holidays. It's your business so it's entirely up to you! Just make sure to be fair across the board, and of course, don't discriminate.

Chapter 20
Payments

Covered in this chapter

- Deposit and Final Payment
- Payment by Checks
- Credit card Payment
- PayPal Payment

Wahoo! You've chosen a stellar property, you've accurately and persuasively written copy that draws people in, you have photographs on the web that make people think, "I want to stay there!" and you've had some communication, either by phone or e-mail, with a potential guest. Now they want to secure their stay at your place. Payday!

Deposit and Final Payment

Ask any landlord, the best day of the month is payday. For the vacation rental owner, it can come a few times a month. If you own more than one VR, it might become a regular occurrence, as most stays involve two payments, one for the deposit to secure the rental and the final payment. They don't gain access to your home until they have paid in full.

Unlike the landlord, there are no tenants to evict, except in the very rare case of a holdover, where someone outstays what they have agreed to. A copy of the signed contract and a visit from the sheriff will usually take care of that.

One of the many benefits of owning a vacation rental is that your guests don't get to stay unless they have prepaid in full. As the owner, you get to dictate when and how you'll be paid.

So, what are the best ways to get paid?

Beth says, *"Sandra called me one night in a state of panic. 'Beth, I don't think I can do this. Dean just showed me what we paid in credit card fees last year. $18,000! That's a whole car! I think we're going to stop taking credit cards. Offer people a discount for paying with a check."*

I could see that a number that high in fees was an emotional trauma for Sandra. What else could she do with $18,000? Fund the boys' college education, buy a car, new furniture for all the cottages, a trip around the world? Tempting, but I knew that removing credit cards from their business would do more harm than the $18,000 they would save. Removing the quick and safe credit card payment option from their business would turn many people away and result in a loss of income. It would also create extra man hours as checks would need to be picked up from the post office, logged in the appropriate place, deposit slips filled out, additional trips to the bank, and then additional communication for confirmation of the reservation. For 15 cottages, the margin for error and the additional work load was not something to discount.

Beth said, "Breathe. This is a great thing! Look at it this way. That $18,000 only represents 2-3 percent of your business. The higher the number, the higher your income. Next year, try for

192

$50,000 in credit card fees! Just make sure you're paying the lowest percentage that you can on your transactions, and you'll be fine. What kind of a discount is 2 percent to offer your guests? On $100 night, you would only be offering them a $2 discount. That's not appealing enough to offset your losses and hassle."

Payment by Checks

Checks—there are few benefits and a number of negatives with taking checks. And the few times I've consented to take a check, the percentage of people changing their mind is much higher than when people have paid with a credit card. Once they hit "Submit" on the payment button, people seem to stop shopping and start anticipating their trip. But a verbal or e-mailed agreement to put the check in the mail doesn't seem to stop people from searching for the best rate.

In fact, I was doing some consulting for a competitor and was answering e-mails for them. I had just taken a booking, reluctantly, for a woman who promised to pay via check, the very next morning. Two days later, I was surprised to receive an inquiry from the same woman for the same dates, but this was for the other property. Clearly, even though I had agreed to hold the space and had blocked it off on the calendar, the guest didn't feel the same level of commitment and was still tire kicking. If I hadn't been consulting, I would have never known, and just thought the mail was slow.

Benefits of checks

Once you have the money, you are not subject to charge backs that you can get with credit cards. Every market is different. I have never dealt with charge backs, Sandy has had quite a few.

There is no cost associated with cashing or depositing checks. As long as you have a bank account, you should be able to deposit without penalty. Check to be sure if there is a limit on deposits.

Drawbacks of checks

When is the reservation actually confirmed? When they say they have mailed it, or when you receive it, or when the bank clears the check? And what do you do with the time in the meantime? What if someone else is interested? Is it reserved?

Checks are not as professional as credit cards. To get a merchant account, the bank has to give you an approval. It lends a measure of credibility to your business.

Going to the bank a few times a week can be a hassle and will add to the amount of time you spend on your business each week.

Refunds can be a hassle. Returning deposit checks can be a hassle.

Items really do get lost in the mail. Who pays the stop payment fee if it is lost?

Banks charge both the person who wrote the check as well as the person who deposited or cashed the check a fee if the check is returned for NSF.

The timing of checks makes it a factor. What if you wait a week to do the deposit, and they expected you to cash it last week, and now their account is overdrawn? Big headache.

Payment with Credit Card

Credit Cards—more people than ever today are whipping out their credit card to make payments for travel and everything else. You can do it instantly, either online or over the phone, and the reservation is made, no waiting for the mailman and wondering if the check really is in the mail.

Pros

You open yourself up for much more business than if you only take checks.

People feel a measure of security—if they send you a check, you can cash it and not honor your reservation. If they give you a credit card number, they have a way to dispute the charges should you be a fraudulent operation.

Cons

You pay as little as 2 percent up to 5 percent or higher, with some places you also pay a monthly fee. International transactions are generally an additional 1 percent.

Guests can do a chargeback, and the responsibility is on you to prove the customer owes you the money.

PayPal Payments

One of the best online solutions for processing both checks and instant payments from peoples' online accounts and checking accounts is PayPal. I have used a Merchant Account (which is different from a personal account) for five years now with very few problems.

PayPal is recognized the world over as being a specialist in safe, secure online monetary transactions. People from all over the world, including Vanuatu, Hong Kong, Australia, New Zealand, and Europe and North America have used the system to pay for accommodations in Fiji.

Benefits

Fraud preventions—Scammers hate PayPal. I have had people who I highly suspect are scammers refuse to use PayPal, but practically hop up and down to pay with any other method. They've begged, they've pleaded, they've dangled the prospect of huge bookings and incentives, but they all walk away when I tell them PayPal is the only option.

I can detect a tear in their eye and a catch in their throat as they send me one last e-mail, imploring me to take a cashier's check or credit card through another payment portal. I has never been burned in a scam, although I have detected some.

You never see a credit card number. If their card is lost or stolen and compromised, you don't have to defend yourself as you don't have access to their numbers. You set up a secure payment page, and the client is then sent to PayPal, where the transaction takes place. A few moments later, "Ding" you get an e-mail saying you have a new payment.

You can set it up to authorize a payment, at which point you can review the reservation, and decide whether or not to proceed. If they fill out your reservation form, and you find that it doesn't meet your criteria, for example, you are already reserved or it does not meet your minimum stay requirements, you can release the hold on the funds and politely decline the reservation. As you never had their funds, it's not a binding contract.

PayPal keeps great records that are easy to use in tax time. You can run monthly and yearly reports, as well as for specific times.

The fees are reasonable.

People are familiar with PayPal, and can pay three ways; with the funds currently in their account, with the checking account, or with a credit card. If you have a merchant account with PayPal, your customers do not have to be PayPal members to pay you, they just enter their billing information and use it as a regular credit card processor. If they are PayPal members, it is instant access via entering their password.

Drawbacks

Because PayPal is so sensitive, it sometimes triggers a decline when it's a legitimate payment. In my experience, there are two main reasons this is triggered—the first is when a client mistakenly enters via the wrong selection—either they enter the payment portal through the PayPal member selection and they are not a member, or the reverse. The other thing that triggers a decline is if the client is traveling at the time they make the payment. Thieves often capture credit card information and send it across the world. So, if your client is traveling at the time they are making a payment, it may trigger a decline. These declines, while rare, can be frustrating for both you and the guest.

PayPal holds a rolling reserve of 20 percent. This means on a transaction of $500, they will hold $100 for chargebacks and refunds for two months. This means that 20 percent of your sales will be held for sixty days.

As with any credit card processing system, the fees add up.
Homework:
Research your options, and decide upon your best way to receive payments.

What will be your preferred payment acceptance method and why?

_____

_____

_____

_____

What steps will you have to take to set up procedures?

_____

_____

_____

_____

Chapter 21
Taxes

Covered in this chapter

- Celebrate Taxes
- Income Taxes and Write-Off's
- Local Travel and Tourism Tax
- Room/ Lodging Tax
- Personal Property Tax

Celebrate Taxes

Taxes are a cause for celebration. Why? Because that means that other people paid you for a service you provided, and that you now get to pass some of your earnings along to the government to pay for roads, emergency services, schools, etc. This is a particularly rosy view of what most people dread, but the point is, that making money is a great problem to have. The government doesn't tax (with the exception of property taxes) on simply having a vacation rental, they tax on the profit with income taxes.

As for room taxes, you simply collect the taxes, and once a month supply the forms and payment, proving to the local government that you are a contributing member to the economy.

Income taxes and Write-Offs

Have you wanted to be one of those people who could write off a trip on their taxes? With a vacation home, travel to your second home is a legitimate expense. Of course, there are limitations, so check with your accountant. Other expenses many vacation rentals can write off are:

Depreciation
Advertising
Utilities
Mortgage interest
Furniture
Appliances
Linens
Cutlery
Cleaning supplies
Wages
Repairs
Mileage

Local Travel and Tourism Tax

Each city is different; however, most collect a room tax from any business that provides accommodations. The average rate is around 4 percent of the total sale. Your local government will be delighted to speak to you about it.

Room and Lodging Taxes

For lodging taxes, you will set your price, and the taxes are added onto it. For example, if your rates are $100/night, and your state and local taxes are 13 percent, then the rate is $113. You haven't lost any money in paying state and local taxes. In fact, you've done something very good. You're collecting $13 from your guests, just like a hotel would, and contributing to tourist features in your area. You are now a contributing member of your tourist community and supporting the vacation rental industry.

Recently, hotels have begun banding together to make vacation rentals illegal in certain areas. They are feeling the growth of the industry and they don't like it, and they are taking it to city council meetings all over the country. Often, these hotels are friendly with the elected officials who make the final decision. By faithfully paying taxes, you show that your industry, the vacation rental industry, is a contributing force in the economy. A list of taxes that you have collected on behalf of the city or the county will go a long way in giving your concern legitimacy in the eyes of the local and state government.

Personal Property Tax

Many cities also charge tax on the personal property you use in your business such as furniture, kitchen items etc. The tax is usually very small. Check with your local tax office for details. If you fail to pay there can be substantial penalties and interest.

Homework

Check with your local government and find all of the taxes that will need to be added on to your accommodation rates.

_____

_____

_____

_____

_____

Chapter 22
Constructing Your Welcome Packet

Covered in this chapter

- When and Why to Send Your Welcome Pack
- What to Include in the Welcome Packet
- Two Examples of Welcome Packets

Welcome Packets are sent after final payment has been received and cleared. Another payday! It's a cause for excitement for both the guest, who is about to take a vacation, and for you, who has more money in the bank. Since it will include the address and information on how to enter your property, it should not be sent before this time.

When and why to send your Welcome Packet

Guests eagerly await the Welcome Packet. It's exciting for them and they are getting insider information on their new home away from home. Their much anticipated trip is getting close!

There's a second reason the Welcome Packet is so important; it's a huge help for you. Ideally, your Welcome Packet should cover everything a guest would have questions about. This will minimize the amount of calls and e-mails you will have to answer.

This is a living document, you will add onto it and change it as you get questions from people you hadn't thought to include in earlier copies, or if something changes, like changing from gas logs to a wood burning fireplace.

I create the Welcome Packet in Microsoft Word, customizing the first page with the guests' names, arrival dates, times, and check out dates and time. This way, should there be any error, there is enough time to deal with an emergency Plan B.

Because it's twenty pages, I convert it to an Adobe PDF and send it as an attachment.

Since Fiji is a foreign destination, people are very eager for information on electricity, water, etc. The flight time ranges from four hours to eleven hours, so it's good fodder for leafing through on the airplane. A welcome packet for a familiar destination does not need to be that long.

Sandra's Welcome Packet is less expansive than mine. It includes separate documents for directions and key code and an additional document for the property itself, amenities she offers as well as links to the area for the guest to plan their stay. She sends a customized cover letter to each guest with the attachments. Sandra's properties are all located in the States and most of her guests travel from the same coast between ten and two hours to the destination by car. They are familiar with the culture, shopping, climate and topography, and require far less explanation on general living conditions. She also uses Adobe's free PDF format to generate the file.

Using Adobe's free PDF format is good for three reasons.

- It's a smaller file—so e-mailing it is easy, especially if you include graphics like maps or photos. It won't clog peoples' inboxes.

- Once it's converted, you can't easily change it. This is important, as you should include check in and checkout dates and times, so everyone is clear.

- Everyone with a computer, be it a Mac or a PC, whether you are running Internet Explorer or Linux, Word or Word Perfect, Windows Vista or Microsoft 1997, can open a PDF. Adobe offers free downloads, and it's recognized and respected worldwide. Newer versions of Word enable you to "Save As" a PDF right from your menu screen.

What to include in a Welcome Packet?

- Customize the first page—welcoming the guests, stating arrival and departure information, INCLUDING times. This way, if they are supposed to check out at 10 a.m., and housekeeping shows up at 10:05, there's no confusion—it's in black and white. Keep a copy of their Welcome Packet on file until after they check out.

- Address—as many people will be using GPS to get to your property, if there is some details, such as one-way streets or off-street parking they need to know about, make sure you spell it out carefully here.

- How to get keys—lock box code (and where the lock box is located.)

- Phone number—if your property has a phone, include it so they can give it to friends and family. Increasingly, with most people having cell phones, VR's don't always have a phone. Make sure they know if you don't have one before booking.

- Phone number to reach staff—they need to be able to reach someone throughout their stay.
- Items provided at the house—linens, CD player, bikes, laundry soap, etc.
- Suggested things for them to bring—sun block, bug spray, etc.
- Expectations—are they expected to take the trash out? Put the linens in the washing machine? The vacation rental industry has had powerful growth in the last few years. Many guests staying now are first timers—and expect a hotel like experience with more room. If you don't provide that, be up front on your website (play it up that it keeps costs down) and in your Welcome Packet.
- Rules—such as where to park, no swimming after 10 p.m.; that they are expected to adhere to.
- Things that aren't obvious—if your laundry room is a unit in a closet in the basement, include that here.
- Anything that you might get a call on.
- Map of the local area with written directions how to get to major attractions AND find their way home—not everyone has a GPS.
- Map of touristy areas—this could be downtown, hiking trails, or anything else that a guest would find useful in their exploration of the area.
- Where your Welcome Book is located.

Two Examples of Welcome Packets

Sample Welcome Packet—Starfish Blue

Welcome to Starfish Blue

Bula!

Welcome to (guest's name.) Happy Honeymoon! (or other special occasion.) The staff is busy making sure everything is wonderful for your holiday and eagerly awaiting your arrival. We have you arriving after 4 PM on October 7, 2015, and departing by 10 AM October 18, 2015. Enjoy your holiday at Starfish Blue, on Fiji's friendly Suncoast.

Our maids come Monday through Saturday. If you would prefer they come less often, or have any special requests, please let us know. We want you to have a wonderful holiday.

Vinaka Vakalevu,

Beth Carson

Phone Numbers
Fiji's area code is **679**. Here are some phone numbers you might need:
Starfish Blue   xxx xxxx

Jai Ram—Starfish Blue Manager	xxx xxxx	xxx xxxx

Jai is available at any time to help with any problems you may encounter.

Suncoast Tours and Taxis	xxxxxxx
suncoasttours@connect.com.fj	
Dr. Naidu—Rakiraki	xxxxxxx
Namaka Medical Centre	xxx xxxx

Tourist class medical services are available near the Nadi airport in Namaka.

Wananavu Beach Resort	xxx xxxx
VoliVoli Beach	xxxxxxx www.volivoli.com
Tanoa Rakiraki	xxxxxxx
www.tanoarakiraki.com	
Iguana Car Rental Rakiraki	xxx xxxx
iguanarentals@connect.com.fj	
Digicel—problems with internet	xxx xxxx
Police	xxx xxxx
Emergency —917	
Fire	xxxxxxx
Emergency —911	
Ambulance	xxxxxxx
Emergency —911	

Note: The last *4k's of roads require a 4 wheel drive. To have a relaxing start to your holiday, we suggest having Suncoast Taxis and Tours pick you up from the airport. While at Starfish Blue, you can either rent a 4 wheel drive vehicle from Iguana Car Rental in Rakiraki on an as-needed basis, or use Suncoast Taxis and Tours.*

Driving Directions—Arriving on your own.

(Directions from the airport)Turn right down the drive, you're home!

Getting places from Starfish Blue

Wananavu Beach Resort is about a five minute drive or a five to ten minute walk. To walk, go up the driveway and turn right. After the residential area, you'll see a small white house with a porch—follow on the road behind that house up the path and over the chain. You'll end up by reception. To go to the marina you can follow the same path, instead going down after you pass the small house. If it's low tide, you can walk along the water's edge. At dark, you'll want a torch (flashlight) provided at the house.

Nananu-I-Ra—you can take a boat from Wananavu's marina. You may want to phone ahead to make sure the boat is available. If Wananavu is closed, you can hire a boat for FJD$200 for the day to take you on a tour and spend time on some of the beaches.

Volivoli Beach—drive up to the top of the development, and turn left at the gatehouse. At the T intersection by the soccer field, turn right. After about five minutes, you'll see the signs for Volivoli on the right.

Town—to get to Town from Starfish Blue, turn left at the drive, left at the top of the hill at the intersection with the guard house, left at the next intersection, and at the main road, turn right. After going through the village there will be a fork in the road at a gas station, take the left.

Tonoa Rakiraki—just before the village, the Tanoa Rakiarki will be on your right.

Tomb of UdreUdre—follow directions to town, but instead, at the fork where town veers off to the left, bear right, and it's on the left.

Church of the Black Christ—go to the main road, and instead of going right towards town, go left, and it's about a twenty minute drive. Look for the signs for St. Francis Xavier Church on the right.

Things to know...

Jai Ram is the Starfish Blue manager. Wananavu will not be able to help you if there is a problem or need at the house.

Resort Privileges—Wananavu Beach Resort is very gracious and offers our guests privileges at the resort. The first day you would like to go to Wananavu, you should introduce yourself at the front desk and give them a credit card for anything you might purchase while there—food, drinks, internet connection, day trips, etc. You'll be given a folio number like their other guests and can charge things to your account. You'll need to check out before leaving and settle your account. Of course, you're very welcome just to use the pool and beach and not purchase anything, but the credit card policy is the same— you'll just have a zero balance at the end.

Occasionally, Wananavu rents out the entire resort to private parties, like weddings or corporate events. The resort is closed to all outside guests during these times. We are not always made aware of these times, and apologize for any inconvenience this may cause. If your stay coincides with one of these times, Volivoli Beach will still be open to you.

Wananavu has nominal charges for non-resort guests for certain things, such as a FJD$5 half day kayak rental, etc. See page below for rates in Fijian Dollars.

Volivoli Beach is a beautiful resort with a large pool, one of Fiji's prettiest beaches and a reasonably priced restaurant with Western style and local food. They welcome our guests—their only request is that you make some purchase while there—a drink, a meal, diving, etc.

Water—Water, water, everywhere and not a drop to drink. We rely on rain water for our house. You might think being surrounded by water that there is plenty. However, here on the Suncoast it is very, very precious. We can go months without rain. If you'd like to go green and get into island living, conserve water whenever possible.

Air Conditioning—We've installed powerful air conditioners in all of the bedrooms for your comfort. The rooms only take about five to ten minutes to cool down once you turn the air conditioner on. Feel free to use them when you're in the room. Of course, please don't run the air conditioners with the windows or doors open or when you're not there. We do have terrific tropical breezes, and many people find the sound of the ocean and the breeze through the palms is very nice for sleeping and they don't use the air conditioning at all.

There is a trick to the air con remotes. When changing the setting, you have to hear a "beep" to know that your request has been transmitted to the machine. If you didn't, continue pressing until you hear the "beep" in conjunction with the action you want.

Note the "Swing" feature. It can swing back and forth, distributing air in a cycle. Or, you can set it to be fixed, either pointing the air down or across or in the middle. Move the digital remote to the swing function, and activate it at the point you want in the cycle to stop it. For example, if you want it blowing down, activate the button when the vents are facing down.

The morning sun comes in the front of the house and we have fantastic sunrises. We have installed insulated curtains throughout the house. Unless the doors are open, which is a great way to catch the breezes, closing the curtains at night will keep the sun from warming the room in the morning. When you're away, you might want to close the curtains in all of the rooms to keep the sun out.

Washer and Dryer—We do have a washer and dryer and if it's not raining, your laundry can dry in about an hour on the line out back in the sunshine. Our maids will be happy to hang your laundry outside for you. If you do need to use the dryer, please leave the wash room curtains open, as the dryer vents back into the closet and it will run continuously.

Safe—We provide a safe in the laundry room. Please utilize it for your valuables. Fiji is a poor nation, and it's best to leave temptation out of sight. We cannot be responsible for money or valuables left around.

Generator—Even on the mainland of Fiji, we do have occasional power outs. We have provided a generator for your comfort. The key is hanging near the back door, and the generator is out the back, second door on the right. It's a good idea to check out the room in the daylight, in case you need it in the dark.

Note—you can only run one air conditioning unit while the power is out.

To operate:

FIRST—turn the switch on the wall to "OFF."
SECOND—turn the generator on using the key, just like you would a car.
THIRD—flip the black switch on the generator.
FOURTH—once it's fully running, turn the switch on the wall to "Generator."
When the power comes back on:
FIRST—turn the switch on the wall to "OFF."
SECOND-turn the generator off using the key.
THIRD—flip the switch down.
FOURTH—turn the switch on the wall back to "FEA." (Fiji Electrical)
Following these steps could save a life. If a technician is working on the line to repair it, and the generator is turned on without the wall on the switch in the "OFF" position, it could cause electrocution.

OK—we now have the business out of the way, now to the fun stuff.

Shopping—there are four or five grocery stores in Rakiraki and an open air market. Grocery shopping is limited in Rakiraki, in fact, in all of Fiji you will not find the selection you do at home. The best shop is near the airport—take a right instead of a left, and at the first round about, take your first left, and you'll see Courts MegaCentre and New World Market. As of the time of this writing, it is open from 8:30 AM-8:00 PM. Here, you'll find the best selection of items. There is also a grocery store in Lautoka, one block passed the Chili Tree Cafe, where you can find a larger selection of food.

You cannot get beef in Rakiraki, but there is a butcher at the end of Denarau Island in Nadi, as well as Lautoka near the port. Fresh fish and whole frozen chickens are available in Rakiraki. We have a rotisserie oven for the chicken.

There is a Hot Bread store for fresh bread. The fruit and vegetable market is near the bus stop—you purchase things by the bundle or pile. Small bills and coins are the best.

Rakiraki is not a tourist town. You will see real Fijians going about their business. Some popular items to buy are Bula shirts for men, (like Hawaiian shirts.) For women, there are Indian shops that sell beautiful saris. While you may not wear one, they make beautiful wall hangings and gifts. There are also clothes stores that sell Western clothing.

Food Preparation—since Fiji is tropical, there is the need to be careful when preparing and serving food. Crumbs left on the counter are a siren call to ants and there will soon be a conga line of delighted, six-legged creatures happy to have dinner. Thwart them by keeping food put away and the counters clean.

Snorkel Gear—the snorkeling in Fiji is fabulous. Some people snorkel every day. We provided masks and snorkels, but no footwear.

To ensure a good fit, you may want to purchase a set at home and bring it with you. I've found really good deals at Amazon.com.

The water entry is rocky in front of our house, so you'll want your own footwear for snorkeling. There are occasionally stingrays and jelly fish. If you step on a stingray, call Dr. Naidu immediately. To clean snorkel gear—use warm, sudsy water (not bleach.) The maids will clean the gear in between guests.

Places to snorkel—Starfish Blue The area down the steps from our house has great snorkeling, but is very rocky. You will want reef shoes. It's easiest to go at high tide when you can float over most of the rocky bit to the edge of the reef, where the best snorkeling is. This is where you can see the water change color from light to dark. You can swim down to Wananavu. The beach area by Wananavu has a sandy beach for easy access and loungers. If you'd rather not deal with the rocky area, here are a few options.

Wananavu—you could walk to Wananavu and swim from there. Afterwards, you could relax in a lounge chair on the beach.

Nananu-I-Ra—some of the most picturesque beaches in all of Fiji are located a ten minute boat ride away on Nananu-I-Ra Island, called Ra for short. Just walk to Wananavu to the jetty and you can ride over and they will arrange pick up. There is a fee, of course. Check with reception or the marina.

There are many be beaches to choose from on Nananu-I-Ra. One of my favorite places is MacDonald's Backpackers, where they have wooden loungers and hammocks, a pier where they feed the fish every night, and easy beach access for snorkeling. They do not, however, have toilets available for non-guests. It's best to call in advance and let them know you are coming. The fish are very large and docile there and used to inquisitive people.

There are also other parts of the island that offer a deserted island feel—you can be the only ones there and there are no facilities, but a fantastic way to get away from it all. Just ask at Wananavu and they can take you and arrange a return time. If Wananavu is closed, you can hire a local boat.

Day Trip—another option is to do a day trip with Wananavu. Most days they have a snorkel trip, usually around 10:00 AM or so, and they will take you in the boat and drop you off in the water and wait for you.

Volivoli Beach—Volivoli has day trips as well as snorkeling off the beach. You can take the gear from the house as long as you return it before you depart so it is there for the next guests coming in. They also have the only dive shop in the area. They can do full certifications, or a half-day, Introduction to Scuba, where you only go a short distance down—a great way to try it out.

Internet—Wananavu has a computer in the gift shop with internet access for a fee. The gift shop closes at 4 PM, but often they will open it back up for you if you need something. The connection is slow as of this writing.

For those traveling with their own laptop, we offer a starter kit for internet option. We have a USB connector stick, and give you a $20 card for access. This should be enough for casual e-mail checking every few days for up to a week. If you have time left over, feel free to leave the card behind for the next guest. If you need more time online there are places in town to get another card. The connection is slow. I suggest not using the time at the house to send photos, or if you do, send images that are very small, as it will take a long time and has a high likelihood of disconnecting while you are sending. Very frustrating, not what you want on vacation! Wait until you are home, or use Volivoli's internet, it's very fast.

Internet hints for use at Starfish Blue—when you insert the Digicel USB Stick, it will automatically download the software. The first time you use it, under

"Settings" (the one with the tools) highlight "Fiji."

Then, hit "Edit" and verify that the Config Filename is "Fiji" and that the dial number is *99#

Click OK

Click "Set as Default"

Then click on the Connect Button (the one with two arrows)

Click Connect Now

IF YOU HAVE ISSUES, CALL DIGICEL DIRECTLY AT 700 3555. They have technicians available twenty-four hours a day.

Hint—the best reception is in the Master Suite or out on the hanging bed. Reception goes in and out, so while you may have five bars when you log on, it may only last a few minutes. It's best to quickly check your e-mail, then log off and write your e-mail, then log back on. The card goes by data used, so checking e-mail does not use very much data at all, but sending pictures or surfing the internet will use it more quickly. Note—the software does not support Macs.

Power—for our North American guests, power outlets have an added feature. There is a rocker switch on each plug in point, you can turn the power off and on to something plugged in via that switch. So if something is plugged in but not working, check to see if power is turned on where it is plugged in.

If traveling from the U.S. or Canada, Fiji is on a different voltage. We provide converters and adaptors. A converter converts the amount of electricity that will go into your electronic device. They are usually bulky and heavy. An adapter allowed our cords to fit into the different shape of the outlets in Fiji, but do not change the voltage any. We provide both.

Many electronic devices that you would travel with some with their own converters built in. Check the plug to see if it has a range. If it says something like, "110 to 220v" you should not need a converter. When I travel, I do not need a converter, as my laptop, battery charger for my digital camera and camcorder all have converters built into their system. I still need to use an adapter, as the plug won't fit properly into the outlet.

Issues—Jai is a wonderful manager. He can handle most any problem that arises. However, if something is not being dealt with, please send me an e-mail or phone me immediately so I can assist. I love this tiny spot on the globe, and hope you have a perfect holiday. The maids, Rozy and Reshmi, the gardener, Mahen, and Jai are very eager for you to have a great holiday, and will be very helpful if something should go wrong or if I would need to contact them. If you let us know while you are there we will do our best to solve any problems that come up.

Phone—there is a phone for you at Starfish Blue. Local calls are free. For long distance you will need a phone card. You can purchase them in Fiji, or you can buy an international AT&T or other international card for calling home.

Maid Service—depending on the number of people, either one or both of the maids will normally come around 10 AM. The gardener/pool man will come between 8-9 AM. They will all leave around noon. However, please let us know if this does not work for you. Some people would prefer privacy, so if you would rather not have the maids come six times a week, or come at a different time, let us know. The maids are paid by the month, so they will not lose money if you would prefer not to have them come. You can have them come every day, or once a week, or anywhere in between. Just let us know what you would like. They walk home, so if you happen to be leaving around the time they are, they would love a ride, even part of the way.

215

Tipping—while tipping is not expected, it is very much appreciated. To avoid confusion, it's best to hand the tip directly to the person whom you would like to receive it. As you may not see the staff on the day you depart, it's best to do it the day before you leave.

I hope you enjoy a wonderful and relaxing holiday!

Beth Carson
beth.starfishblue@gmail.com

828 XXX-XXXX USA phone

828 XXX-XXXX USA fax

Items provided at Starfish Blue

- All linens and towels, including pool towels
- Washing machine and dryer (Please only use the dryer if it's raining! It vents back into the house making it very hot.)
- All cooking utensils, plates, cutlery, and appliances
- TV, DVD, Satellite connection
- Small selection of DVD's
- Small selection of books
- CD player (bring your favorite CD's)
- Alarm clocks in all rooms
- Snorkel gear (masks and snorkels, bring your own footwear—it's rocky in front of our house)
- Telephone—local calls are free, you'll need a phone card for long distance, even within Fiji
- Converters and adaptors for U.S. cords
- Cords to plug your mp3 players and iPods to the stereo system and a CD player upstairs

We have made every effort to consider all of your needs and hope that everything goes smoothly. However, we cannot guarantee any of our appliances or features, please let us know immediately if there is a problem so we can get it fixed as soon as possible.

Just a note, since Fiji is a tropical island, you'll see some locals around the house—geckos, which are lovely because they eat bugs, and the odd insect. If you see more than that, phone Jai so he can get the pest control people out. They come on a regular basis, but it is a tropical island. You'll see frogs at night outside.

Speaking of nights, if it's a clear night, the stars pop. Turn off most of the house lights and sit in a lounge chair for a nearly panoramic view of the stars.

Issues? We are here to help!

You have taken time away from your busy life, traveled a great distance, and are in a new environment. We want you to go home perfectly relaxed and with happy memories of Fiji and Starfish Blue.

If you encounter a problem, please let us know immediately so it doesn't disturb your enjoyment of this much anticipated holiday. I promise you that we want to know should something not meet your expectations, and we will do everything we can to correct the problem as soon as possible. The only problems we ignore are the ones we don't know about.

The Starfish Blue employees are well-trained and eager to please. No one will take offense if you let them or me know that something could be better. By letting us know, you are giving us the opportunity to correct the problem. We appreciate it.

What to do if there is a problem:

Contact Jai as soon as you can. Jai knows the repair people to call and can fix many issues immediately. Call any time, day or night if there is a problem.

Jai— Mobile XXX XXXX

Home XXX XXXX

If that doesn't meet your satisfaction, contact me. I have Skype and receive e-mails immediately on my cell phone. I am easy to reach and eager to help facilitate the resolution to any problem. I will contact you very quickly if I miss your call. Problems are rare, but when they happen on your holiday, we want to know immediately.

Vinaka Vakalevu,

Beth Carson
beth.starfishblue@gmail.com
828 XXX-XXXX USA cell
828 XXX-XXXX USA phone
828 XXX-XXXX USA fax
Pages of activities and local information follow.

Sample Cranmore Cottages Welcome Packet

Welcome to Cranmore Cottages

Grey Oak Cottage

XXX Millard J. Dr. Hendersonville, NC

We know you have a choice and we are delighted to have the opportunity to serve you as our guest!

The following pages contain information that you may find helpful in navigating your cottage and your stay. Should you need any further assistance please do not hesitate to contact any of our Cranmore staff as we are always pleased to help any way we can.

Kind Regards,

Sandra Cloer
Owner
Cranmore Cottages
828-XXX-XXXX personal cell

Check In

We have a self-check in with the key code you will find on your direction sheet under the address of your cottage. You will find a lock box to the left of the front door. Punch in your code and pull the small black lever at the top down to release the fob. You will find a key inside to let yourself in. You will find keys inside to carry with you. <u>We suggest that you keep the extra key in the fob so that you never accidentally lock yourself out of your cottage</u>. You must clear the old code out (with the second black lever) in order to punch the code in once again to replace the fob. *Please do not change the code on the lock box.*

Check in is at 4:00 p.m.. I am sorry, but we cannot provide for early check in. Subject to availability you can make prior arrangements to reserve your cottage for a half day beginning at 8:00 a.m. for an additional cost of $65. We will not have a guest stay the prior evening.

CANCELATION POLICY

We cannot refund for any reason should you need to cancel within thirty days of your stay. We encourage you to consider trip insurance should something unexpected come up for you. Our family uses www.insuremytrip.com but I am sure there are many companies out there that offer the service.

If you cancel prior to thirty days of your stay we will retain $100 of your deposit and refund the rest.

CHECK OUT

Check out is at 10:30 a.m.. We ask you to do a few things to help us expedite readying the cottage for the next guest's arrival.

~Please strip your beds of sheets and place them at the foot of the bed.

~Please put your tied bags of trash in the trash can outside located to the right of your cottage.

~Please wash your dishes and put them away.

~Please clean out the fridge of any leftover food.

~Please start a load of <u>towels</u> before you leave.

~Leave your keys on the kitchen table.

~If your stay is during the summer months, please set the air conditioner at 74 upon departure. If your stay is during the winter months, please set the heat at 50. We ask that you turn off all lights and televisions upon departure.

~Please lock the door behind you.

FOR YOUR COMFORT

Your cottage has a central air heat pump. We have had very unseasonably hot and cold weather the past year. Should you feel too cold you will find extra space heaters in the hall closet. Should you need extra fans during the summer months, please let us know and we will be happy to provide them for you as well.

KEYS

Your security is important to us. We provide two sets of keys for your party to carry with you. There is also a key located in the lock box at the front door. We encourage you to leave the key in the lock box at all times so that you never accidentally lock yourself out of the cottage. Always scramble the key code after replacing the key back in the fob.

Should you lose a key during your stay please let us know immediately so it can be replaced. If you take one or more keys with you upon departure there is a $100 re-lock fee that will be charged to your credit card.

WE PROVIDE FOR YOUR CONVIENCE

~A fully equipped kitchen including but not limited to: coffee maker, bean grinder, microwave, slow cooker, pots & pans, casserole dishes, baking dishes, pizza pan, cake pan, muffin pan, cookie sheet, dishes, glasses, wine glasses, wine bottle opener, can opener, cooking utensils, and serving bowls.

~Television, DVD player, CD stereo, iPod dock, and a variety of movies on DVD.

~All linens and towels.

~Washer & Dryer, Iron & ironing board.

~Dish soap, hand soap, laundry supplies, cleaning supplies, paper towels, trash can liners, toilet paper, and coffee filters.

~Charcoal grill and grilling tools. There is usually charcoal and starter fluid in the cottage; however, you may want to check this before you plan a grilled meal.

~Extra fans and space heaters.

PET FRIENDLY

We are happy to be a pet friendly cottage. If you have made prior arrangements to bring your pet with you, we ask that you follow these simple guidelines: Never leave your pet alone in the cottage unless it is properly crated. No pets are ever allowed on the furniture or bedding. Should we see that your pet has been on either an $80 cleaning fee will be charged to your credit card. Please clean up your pet's waste by bagging it and putting it in the trash can outside. We ask that you vacuum before you depart.

FIREPLACE USE

You have a wood burning fireplace in your cottage. If you have made arrangements to purchase firewood through Cranmore you will find it located to the right of your cottage in the locked wood bin. Please use the code you have received to unlock the bin to gather your wood and starter logs. Please relock the bin when you have finished gathering your wood.

There is supposed to be soot in the fireplace. It is very difficult to start a fire in a clean fireplace. Please do not over build the fire. Never leave a fire unattended by going to bed or leaving the cottage.

We also ask that you do not leave candles burning unattended.

There are smoke detectors around the house as well as a carbon monoxide detector. Please do not remove the batteries as they are there for your safety.

You will find a fire extinguisher beside the washing machine in the laundry room. <u>If there is a fire call 911 FIRST.</u>

CABLE TV AND INTERNET SERVICES

There is no password to the internet in your cottage so you should have no problem connecting. The router is located to the left of the television. Should you have difficulty connecting, disconnect the router for sixty seconds and reconnect it. This should cause it to boot up again.

You have expanded basic cable services. The cable box must be on as well as the television in order to receive signal. If you are having trouble with cable connection please check first to be sure your TV is on the correct input and then be sure that it is on channel 3. Be sure your cable box is on as well.

TRASH PICK-UP

Trash is picked up on Wednesday. You do not need to take the trash to the curb. All trash must be in a tied trash bag in the can. There is a fee for leaving loose trash in the can

If you need the trash removed before Wednesday because it is overflowing please call 828-XXX-XXXX and we will have staff come and take care of it.

YARD WORK

Your yard will be mowed on Thursday during the season. We may have staff doing other yard work during other days of the week as well. If we need to do other yard work we will phone you to let you know or send you a text message.

SNOW

When it snows we hire removal for the driveway. We have them put us on a priority list but actually have no control as to when they show up. We will have staff come to shovel your steps and walk way. Please let us know if your steps become icy during your stay so we can address it immediately. We do leave a shovel and rock salt in the laundry room should you need it.

MAINTENANCE ISSUES

We welcome maintenance calls. We want your stay to be as pleasant as possible for you. Letting us know something isn't working properly is helpful to us. We will have maintenance address the issue as soon as possible. You can call or text Dwight, maintenance supervisor, directly at 828 XXX-XXXX. You can always reach Sandra at 828-XXX-XXXX and I will pass the work order on to Dwight.

Maintenance will be wearing a Cranmore Cottages t-shirt and will leave a sheet in your cottage or taped to your door regarding what was addressed and the time frame they were there should you not be in while they are servicing your cottage.

Occasionally something will break that we need to call another service provider in to fix for us. We always ask to be a priority with these companies but ultimately are not in control of how quickly they will accommodate us. Please know we are doing everything we can to resolve the issue as quickly as possible.

HOUSEKEEPING

We do not provide ongoing housekeeping through the week. If you would like for housekeeping to come in and clean mid-week we can do that for an additional fee of $45. This will include linen change of all beds, clean towels, cleaning the bathroom, cleaning the kitchen, dusting, vacuuming, sweeping, and mopping the floors.

SMOKING

All of Cranmore Cottages' properties are non-smoking. Please smoke outside on the porch should you need to. We ask that you are courteous of other guests and clean up all your butts by putting them in a bag in the trash can.

MEDICAL EMERGENCY

Should you have any type of medical emergency please call 911. Your cottage address is XXX Millard J. Dr. Hendersonville, NC. The closest hospital is Pardee Hospital off of 64 east. It is about one mile away. There is a large medical and trauma center located in Asheville called Mission Hospital.

CLOSEST GROCERY AND DRUG STORES

Make a right out of your drive on to Millard J. Drive. Follow it to the stop sign and make a right onto Glasgow Ln. Follow to the stop sign and make a right onto Brevard Rd. (64 west). Go approximately one-quarter mile and you will see the Laurel Park Plaza on your right.

Located in that plaza is a small Ingles Grocery Store, Right Aid Drug Store, ABC Liquor Store and several small cafes and bistro.

To get to Wal-Mart follow same directions to Glasgow Ln. but at the stop sign make a right onto Brevard Rd (64 east). Follow 64 east for five miles and you will see the Wal-Mart Plaza on your left. There is also a Sam's in that plaza, Radio Shack, Pier One, and several clothing and shoe stores. You will find an O'Charlie's Restaurant, Atlanta Bread Restaurant, Zaxby's Restaurant and a Chinese Restaurant in that plaza.

There are many chain restaurants and a small mall on Four Seasons Boulevard on your way to Wal-Mart.

TO PLAN YOUR STAY

A helpful site for planning your stay is www.historichendersonville.org. There you will find a calendar of events, listings of local activities and listings of all of our lovely shops and restaurants. For planning your waterfall hikes go to www.visitwaterfalls.com and you will find a complete listing of trail maps.

ELIJAH MOUNTAIN GEM MINE & FIREFLY ANTIQUES

Elijah Mountain Gem Mine and Firefly Antiques are Cranmore Cottages' business. Visit the mine and tell them you are a Cranmore Guest and you will receive a complimentary Little Miner Bucket for your party. You will also receive 10 percent off in the rock shop and Firefly Antiques. Go to www.elijahmountain.com for directions, hours of operation, and coupons.

Optional Amenities for Your

Pleasure and Indulgence

Wine & Cheese $39.00

One lovely bottle of wine accompanied by a seasonal selection

of cheese, crackers, fruit, and nuts.

Champagne & Strawberries $39.00

A decadent and romantic treat for you and the one you love.

Roses $29.00

A classic; there simply is no better way to say, "I love you."

Firewood & Starter Logs Delivered $29.00 —$49.00

Seasoned firewood with starter logs waiting conveniently at your doorstep. Comes in two sizes: three evening package or seven evening package. There is nothing better than to snuggle up by a crackling fire on a crisp mountain evening.

Any of the above delights can be added to your stay prior to arrival.

To order: send us an e-mail at cranmorecottages@gmail.com *or call 888/868-1779.*

Luxurious Therapeutic Massage

By Licensed Massage Therapists David Freeman & Sallina Freeman

Enjoy the luxury of a therapeutic table or chair massage provided at your cottage. Licensed Massage Therapists David and Sallina Freeman use integrative techniques for stress, muscle tension relief, and range of motion issues.

Individual or Couples Massage Available

David Freeman, NCL #6659
Sallina Freeman, NCL #6658
60 Minutes – $85.00 per person
(Additional minutes —$1.00 per minute)
To schedule a massage at your cottage, call us at 888 XXX XXXX.

Chapter 23
The Guest Book

Covered in this chapter

- Guest Book Function
- What to Include in Your Guest Book
- How to Find Area Information

Your Guest Book is a living document, and one of the first things a guest will check out when they arrive at your home. It's the transition from their dependency to you on the phone and via e-mail, and being able to live out their vacation on their own. The best Guest Books have both the guests and the owner in mind, it should dramatically minimize the need for them to contact you.

Guest Book Function in the Home

The Guest Book is part home owner's manual, part hotel concierge, and part insider's tips to your favorite vacation spot. It's critical that it be compiled in an organized manner and be neat. It is a key component in your guests' satisfaction. By doing a few hours work to put a professional looking book together, you'll make a fabulous first impression and save yourself many interrupting phone calls.

To help your guest navigate the property more easily, include in the first pages the most important information and move toward information that isn't as urgent for them to know but may need. Using dividers is a nice way to help them locate the information they are looking for. Use a stylish binder or have one made at www.zazzle.com .

Laminate your pages using a nice grade of paper or slide the pages into a protective sheet so they don't become soiled or torn.

Your Guest Book not only makes life easy on your guests, it should make life easy for you. Let's take a peek at a guests' first hour in a vacation rental.

Imagine a guest who's been traveling for a few hours to get to your VR. Maybe they worked a full day, then spent the rest of the evening in the car. They arrive and are able to access the keys and walk into their new home for the weekend. On first impression, they are very pleased. They notice the fresh smell, the clean carpets, the well equipped kitchen, and put their bags in the bedroom. Back in the living room, all they want to do is stretch out and mindlessly flip channels before they go back out again. Maybe they plan on staying in and ordering carry out for a late dinner.

Hmm. After searching all surfaces in the living room and tearing up the couch, they find the remote in the cushions. Ahhh, finally. Now, they hit the power button, and they watch the green light on the satellite box go off and on, but no picture comes on the screen. After much searching, they find another remote. What button to push on this one? OK, this is a big job.

They put down the remotes and look for the Guest Book. The three worn pages stapled together are sorely outdated. No instructions on how to work the TV. No restaurant suggestions or directions. No coupons. No easy dinner in for them.

Sighing, our tired and hungry guests look for the phone book. After a frustrating search, they find it in a desk drawer in the second bedroom. They look through the many pages of restaurants. Which serves the area they are in? Which has great food? The phone book doesn't make sense to the couple, because they aren't locals, and don't recognize street names and neighborhoods.

How are they feeling about your vacation rental? They've been there an hour, but have they rested? Enjoyed their first hour in your home? Or do you think they will start noticing other irritations that they might have not paid attention to. Maybe the driveway is steeper than they are used to, or the rooms are smaller than at home. Maybe the stove is electric and they are used to gas.

Your Guest Book can help shape the way they think about your home and how often they need to call you or feel helpless. Since you don't want them to either feel helpless or have the need to phone you three or four times in one hour, try to anticipate all of their questions.

What to include in Your Guest Book

Welcome Letter

This is a way to warm up a book that could feel very cold and impersonal. Personally sign this page. Then, include page information for each section.

Emergency information

☐ Address of the property in case of emergency. This is especially important as people are increasingly relying on cell phones. They may have your address keyed into their GPS, but if their spouse is having a heart attack, don't count on them to figure that out.

- ☐ How to contact emergency personnel—not every country uses 911

- ☐ Emergency procedures—such as what to do if a snow storm or hurricane is coming

- ☐ Where the closest hospital or trauma unit is with phone number and address

- ☐ Where the closest walk-in clinic is located with phone number and address

- ☐ Where your first aid kit is located

- ☐ Closest pharmacy and twenty-four hour pharmacy

- ☐ Where emergency supplies are located in the home, such as flashlights, candles, ice-melt

- ☐ Emergency shut-offs—gas, water, breaker box

Household Systems and Entertainment

- ☐ How to use the AC/Heating system

- ☐ How to use the TV with a picture of the remote diagramming the buttons. Designate a spot for the remotes. If your Guest Book says that the remotes are left on the coffee table, make sure housekeeping makes sure they are there before the next guests arrive. Use one type of remote for your properties—a universal remote. Spend the time to set up all of the components to work with the one remote. Then, have a full page diagram, and give them step by step instructions for using the TV, DVD, satellite or dish network, and anything else that can be controlled with that remote.

- ☐ Password to the internet

- ☐ What to do if the internet goes out—often, if the internet goes out, it can be fixed by resetting the box. Tell them where the box is located (I stayed at a home where the box was in a kitchen cabinet above the microwave. This involved a housewide search and a call to the owner. Tell them how to unplug and reset it.)

- ☐ How to work the DVD player

- ☐ How to work the CD player

- ☐ How to use their mp3 player or iPod on your stereo system—an increasingly common amenity, the ability to bring for guests to bring their own music and plug it into your system is a favorite among guests. Often, the stereo will need to be turned to "Auxiliary" or something else, so spell this out.

- ☐ How to use the hot tub—hot tubs are a polarizing amenity—owners hate them and vacationers love them. Tell them how to remove the cover, how to work the buttons, and how to replace the cover.

- ☐ How to use the gas log fireplace or fireplace or outdoor fire pit. Diagrams are nice here as well for the gas logs.

Rules and Guidelines

- ☐ Pet policies

- ☐ Smoking policies

- ☐ Check out procedures

- ☐ Condo or HOA rules and regulations, as they apply to the guest

Maintenance Guidelines

- [ ] When to expect yard and pool work—don't have any work before 10 AM unless you have the guests' approval.

- [ ] When to expect housekeeping or how to request additional housekeeping and cost.

- [ ] What to do if a maintenance issue comes up.

- [ ] Location of maintenance supplies in the house and what your tool box includes—Light bulbs, plunger etc.

- [ ] Details about trash pickup.

Area Information

- [ ] Closest Grocery store

- [ ] Closest Liquor store

- [ ] List of shopping

- [ ] List of restaurants

- [ ] List of theaters

- [ ] List of churches

- [ ] Where to find the welcome center in your area

- [ ] Calendar of events—update at least quarterly

What else can you think of that is appropriate for your house?

_____

_____

How to Find Area Information

Look at the types of information you have in your book. How will your guests find what they are looking for? Often, your local visitor center will have information on area events, restaurants, shops, galleries, outdoor activities, and more. Simply print off this information. Highlight your personal and family favorites, adding a personal touch for your guests.

Use lots of "white space." When people look through a Guest Book, generally, they are skimming for specific information. Consider devoting one page to each section—one large picture of the remote (you have a universal one, don't you?) one page on recommended restaurants, one for contact information, etc. Use a large font to write the title, and bullet points or indentations for each new piece of information.

Professional Level Tip—now that you've handled all of the basics, consider adding a warm page written with the information you'd tell your best friend if she were visiting. Give them your favorite restaurants, walks, art galleries, places that locals might only know about. Maybe there's a great massage school in your area, and they take reservations at bargain basement prices. Or an art gallery that has a back room with discounted original art work. Be a source of insider information and update this regularly. No one wants to head out and find a big "Closed" sign.

Homework—take a look through Zazzle's array of three ring binders, and consider a custom binder, with a beautiful photo of your home or area, and name of your house. Binders cost about $25, and are a way to set you apart from other places they've stayed. Other options are leather binders for an executive feel, or to save a few dollars, get a regular three ring binder and insert large photos front and back.

Chapter 24
Customer Service
With Sandra Cloer

Covered in this chapter

- Responding to inquiries
- Under Promise and Over Deliver
- The Basics
- Good Service with Guest Complaint
- Training Employees to Provide Fantastic Guest Service

We are a service industry rather than a product based service. In order to actually have people stay in your homes you must interface with your prospective guest at some point. That is where your customer service begins.

Responding to inquiries

Many of your inquires will begin by e-mail. They will see your listing on a listing portal and send you a message. Likely, they have sent at least eight or ten of this same information requests out to many VR owners at the same time. How you respond is the first clue as to what type of customer service your guest will be receiving.

First, respond promptly. Don't wait for your competitor to show them they are ready to serve when called on. YOU be that person. When the e-mail comes in answer it. If you have a smart phone, utilize the ability to reply as soon as an e-mail hits.

Next, thank them for their inquiry to your property. That sounds simple, but remember they have a lot of choices out there in a growing industry. Thank you goes a long way. Then, answer completely and competently all of their questions. Check your spelling and grammar. Use complete sentences. You want your guest to know you are a professional and take your business seriously.

You may have your initial inquiry by phone. Answer the phone with a smile on your face and your guest will hear it. Listen to what they are saying to you so that you can answer their questions thoroughly and completely. Listen for the REASON they are going on vacation and tell it back to them so they feel a connection with you.

Here is an example of a conversation Sandra had with a perspective guest.

"You're coming for your annual girls chocolate fest? How fun! Have you been doing this for many years? How did it get started? Let me tell you about the best chocolate shop in our area. If you like I can have some waiting for you and your friends on arrival."

I have just set myself apart from the crowd. I care about why they are coming and have even offered to help with having chocolates delivered for their arrival. Great customer service sets me apart. I got the booking.

Under Promise and Over Deliver

Be candid with your perspective guest about what your property offers. Do not over promise and under deliver, there is no greater kill joy than that! If your property requires a four wheel drive to access be sure they understand that. If your view is of your neighbor's fence do not say long range views (if you stand on the roof!).

Once at your home be sure your guest has a way to reach you or your property manager should there be any concerns. Nothing is more frustrating than not being able to reach someone when you need them. Offer several contacts so your guests are never left to fend for themselves should something come up.

Sandra: *"A couple of years ago my husband and I decided to spend a month at the beach with our children during the off season. We were all very excited! We were staying on an island that was about a 30 min drive from the mainland, so we purchased our groceries on our way in to the property. We had a lot as we were going to be staying quite a while.*

Once we arrived we found the lock box broken and we couldn't get into our house. The temperature was in the upper nineties and humidity was high. We had been driving for 8 hours and were all cranky and ready to be inside.

I called the VR owner and could not reach her on her cell or home line. I called again and again leaving message after message. Our kids were hot and tired and our frozen food melted. An hour went by, then another ½ hour. It was then my husband took matters into his own hands and broke into the house himself. Not a very good start to a long stay.

After two hours the owner called me back telling me that she had been having trouble with the lock box for a while now, and she was sorry. Bad answer. Now I see that she wasn't up on the maintenance of the property and wondered what else I would encounter during our extended stay."

If you try to think of it in terms of how you would like to be treated on your vacation this will help you get in the right mind set.

The Basics

Don't have the yard work scheduled prior to 10:30. Do understand your guests are on vacation and trying to sleep in.

Don't schedule regular maintenance during morning hours. Do schedule for the afternoon when your guest will likely be out. Even better? Schedule it for an empty day, or if you have to have work done while they are in your home, ask when is a good time for them.

Don't let a guest's concern go unspoken to. It makes them feel like you don't care. Do tell them how you are going to address their concern and the time frame it will be taken care of.

Don't let a guest show up and be surprised something they are expecting isn't going to be working properly. If you know the hot tub is down don't wait until the guest shows up and figures out it isn't working. Do call ahead and let them know of the trouble and compensate them if necessary.

Good Customer Service with a Guest Complaint:

When a guest calls with a complaint LISTEN TO THEM. They are your best resource in knowing what the market is thinking about your property. An issue handled properly can actually develop a stronger bond with a client and increase the chances of a repeat visit then a mediocre stay with no calls or complaints.

Training Employees to Provide Fantastic Guest Service

Employees

You must develop high guest service skills in your employees.

Train them how to do things you find basic like answering the phone and how to properly fold a towel. Don't assume they will know all the skills you want them to do.

Treat your employees with respect. The same amount of respect you give a guest! They will pass that on to guests if they feel valued as well.

Thank them for a job well done and they will do it again and again. The power of praise is not to be under estimated as a powerful motivator.

Give your staff authority—if you have staff you can trust, consider give them a dollar limit and allow them to deal with some of the issues that you deal with, and cut out the wait time. If the air conditioning isn't working and it's going to be 4 hours until the repair man can fix it, an employee empowered with your authority in that situation to give them a lunch or dinner out can nip negative feelings in the bud. The guests can immediately leave the hot house and go enjoy their afternoon, without any back and forth from you. Of course, the employee will be answerable to you to justify the expense, he can't take a group of friends out to dinner on your dime, but a great employee will rise to the task.

Homework

Contact 3 vacation rentals as a potential guest, and rate their performance. Did you feel welcomed? Or did you feel your inquiry was an inconvenience?

Write your experience here.

_____

_____

_____

_____

Training staff—Think of one thing that your staff is capable of—such as making a call for appliance repair, that your staff can do, train them thoroughly, then see how they do. What's one thing that you could delegate to your staff?

_____

Practice talking with a smile, especially in situations where you are irritated—you can do this in the grocery store, on the phone with the cable company, and see how well you can work through your annoyance and see the person you are dealing with as a person with their own fears and anger.

Chapter 25
The Cranky Guest

Covered in this chapter

- Different Categories of Complaints
- Guest with Legitimate Complaint
- Guest Who Has Had a Bad Day
- Guest Who Will Likely Never be Happy
- Steps for Handling a Guest Complaint

Your most unhappy customers are your greatest source of learning. Bill Gates

We have all had them, a less than satisfied guest or client. Whether you are in the service industry or have a product to sell someone, somewhere, sometime is going to be unhappy. Very, very unhappy. It would be easy for us not to bring the topic up because it can be difficult to address. When you are confronted with an angry guest it can make you feel sickish inside, like you want the earth to swallow you whole.

You may not even sure what you did, because the people before and after these particular guests praised everything about your vacation rental. Maybe it was the weather, maybe their spouse threatened them with divorce during the trip, maybe they got an email letting them know they were fired, and maybe their complaint was legitimate. Who knows, but you are on the receiving end and must decide how to respond. Fortunately, if you have a great product, complaints are few and far between.

Different Categories of Complaints

If you've been in business for any length of time, you've had them. They fall into a few different categories.

Guests with a legitimate complaint.

Guests who have had a bad day and you take the hit.

Guests who are never happy no matter what.

Guest With a Legitimate Complaint

Sometimes it happens. You may double book your property, forget a special amenity that the guest ordered or housekeeping missed that clean by accident. Plan for things to go wrong sometimes because they will. Plan to have a plan for when things go wrong.

Sandra says: *When a guest calls me with a strong complaint I always spend as much time listening to him vent as I can. I do not take what he is saying personally (that can be hard because it is my house with my things) and try to really hear what he is saying to me.*

Then I do this magical thing by making the tiniest of shifts in my mind, it is a small shift but it works. I put myself in my guest's shoes. I try to remember that they likely took this trip without really being able to afford it, have planned for it for a long time, have been traveling for quite some time to get here, are tired and hungry and have other people they are trying to please that are traveling with them. If my house wasn't clean or I was locked out or another guest was in my cottage when I arrived I would be upset too!

By the way, each of those things has actually happened to my guests over the past ten years. Making this shift enables me to generate empathy for my guest and validate their concern.

After you have listened to your guest very carefully and validated their concern, tell them how you plan to deal with the issue and the time frame it is going to take to get it done. Always use a kind and respectful tone. Nobody likes being talked down to.

Say to the guest, "Yes, I understand you are upset about xyz. It would upset me too and I am very sorry that has happened. This is how I am going to take care of it… You can expect maintenance to be here within … Will that work for you?"

Most of the time they will be happy with you taking care of the concern in a timely manner and sometimes they would like some sort of compensation for their trouble.

If it is a situation where the guest must leave the vacation rental in order to fix the concern give them something for their time away. You can pay for their meal while they are out by crediting their account or have Visa gift cards on hand for such an event.

Don't be lulled into complacency by the words "It is okay." It might be, or your guest might be planning a zinger on a review site. Don't wait for them to take the lead, you are the business owner, solve the problem and make them feel good about their perceived loss, even if it costs you a bottle of wine or a meal out. Do a little more than your guest might expect. Go beyond what your competition might do.

If they still insist they are fine still do something special for them. Sandra asks guest if they would prefer a wine a cheese or coffee and pastry and send them which ever they choose.

Follow up the next day making sure everything is still going well for them and let them know you are available should they need anything further. Give them your personal cell if they do not already have it and offer them a discount for the next time they visit with you.

You have effectively touched your guest three times, the last two touches being positive experiences. Handling a bad situation well goes a long way in building the relationship with your guest. If you do a good job your guest is even more likely to return as a repeat guest than if they had an average stay with nothing monumental occurring at all.

The Guest Who Has Had a Bad Day

Sandra: *Last week I got a very short, curt email from one of my guests asking me who gave me the authority to bill any amount to their debit card as they had seen money had been taken out by my company. I wanted to say," Um... YOU. Remember when you filled out the reservation online? You gave me permission then! Remember when you signed and returned the rental agreement to me? You gave me permission once again!"*

My better business sense kicked in and instead I emailed back, explaining to him the billing procedure I used and where he could find those details on the reservation confirmation he was sent as well as the rental agreement he signed and faxed back to me. Then, I moved my cursor to the top of the email and BEGAN the email with telling him how I understood his concern as there is an ever increasing trend toward people stealing others identity. I told him he must be a very thorough person in all he did and that I bet his work and wife appreciated that. I went on to explain our billing process in detail.

He replied saying he was sorry and the billing was fine. My guess is that he was just having a bad day and I took the hit for it. That is ok though, I was able to build him up a little and he felt better about himself AND me.

Once again, begin with taking your ego out of the attack. True, you or your employees may have done nothing wrong to warrant the venomous email or phone call complaint but the important thing is *your guest believes you have.* Give them the courtesy of hearing them out then gently explain where the error is. If you can find a good trait to lift up in them, do so, it will soften their heart towards you and in turn make them more open to what you are going to tell them.

Follow these simple guidelines and you have a happy guest whose opinion of both you and your business will be boosted. If you get angry and defensive, or worse yet patronizing, you will reap long-term damage both to your business and the guest.

The Guest Who Will Likely Never Be Happy

Sandra has a cabin that was built in 1830. It is quirky and added on to. Some of the door ways are short as people were much shorter then and the beams are exposed throughout most of the house. Lights are in odd places as they have been added throughout the years. It is the kind of place you either really love due to the history or do not care for due to the quirks. As candid as she is with the home, some people fail to pick up on the basics, it's age, unusual layout, etc.

A guest called upon arrival. *"Sandra, I do not like this at all. I am not happy."*

"What is the problem? Is there something not working properly? Is the house not clean?" she asks.

"No, everything is fine. It is just, just... really old."

"Well," I told her, "it was built in 1830!"

After moving her to a newly constructed log cabin, she called to say she was not happy there either. *"I had to go down six steps and up five to get into the cabin and it smelled like wood in here."* she said.

Sandra apologized for the wood smell (even though it was made of logs!) and told her she had no other properties available to move her to. The guest sighed at Sandra as if she were putting her out and said she was just going to have to make do with this place. Sandra sent her a wine and cheese tray even though in no way had she done anything wrong, in fact she gone the extra mile doing everything she could for her. A cabin in the mountains was not the experience this guest was looking for, even though that is exactly what she had requested in her inquiry and reserved.

These are the guests you cannot please no matter what you do. No matter how wonderful your company or product, it is not a good match for everyone. The world is too diverse. How else can you explain the cult like devotion some consumers have to anything Apple make, and other consumers who are very frustrated within five minutes of owning one, muttering under their breath as they pack it up to return it. When they get to the store they will give the clerk a piece of their mind. Same computer or iPhone, two polar opposite responses. There wasn't anything wrong with the computer, the consumer just didn't like it.

The best way to avoid this situation is to provide the prospective guest with as much information as possible before they reserve. With all the information they may well eliminate themselves from your calendar. If you are a good listener and ask questions you may be able to cue in to the fact that they will not be happy at your property and you can point them in a different direction.

Now, let's talk as professionals. As we speak to in The Bad Review chapter, there is a very good thing that comes from any complaint. If someone is kind enough to let you know there is a problem, you have a chance of fixing it. These opportunities are like gold. This is your opportunity to problem solve the issue defining exactly what happened, why it happened and how to put specific measures in place to make sure it does not come up again for a future guest. Customer complaints strengthen your business if you let them. A much worse situation is when your guest doesn't mention anything at all, but go home and blast you on the internet.

There is a worst case scenario when your guest has a complaint: they cannot reach someone to tell them they are experiencing a problem. Once again, Sandra has the perfect story to illustrate this.

Sandra: *I had just come back from an overseas trip. We were thrilled to be home and our staff was thrilled to see us. No one could be more happy to have us home than my assistant who had been handling all the emails, phone calls, billing and contracts on her own. She promptly gave me the phone.*

Being in a severe state of jet lag I mindlessly set it on the counter in the kitchen and went to bed. It was only 6pm EST, but it was middle of the night where we had spent the prior three weeks. I slept like a baby until about 4:00 am. I woke up and went to the kitchen to make myself some coffee when I saw my cell phone on the counter. It had over 20 missed calls! I checked and they were all from the same number. I thought I was going to throw up.

A guest had come in late in the evening and could not get in the cottage. Oh, it gets worse. It was January and bitter cold. It gets

249

worse. They were from Florida where it is very warm. Worse yet, it was their wedding night! AHHHHHHHHHH! I got in my car and drove straight down to the cottage to find the two sleeping in their car in the freezing cold!

Does your stomach hurt yet? It should. I let them in their cottage and refunded their entire week long stay. Now your stomach should really hurt.

Each problem is a learning situation. Make sure you have multiple numbers for guests to get in touch with you. Leave these numbers on your voicemail.

Steps for Handling a Guest Complaint

Responding to complaints, negative reviews, or unusual demands takes a bit of finesse. Your knee jerk reaction is to get defensive.

Don't do it.

Don't do it.

Don't do it.

The specifics of how to handle a complaint (no matter which type of complainer you have encountered) properly.

1. Listen to the person with the concern. Do not interrupt what they are saying. Give them your complete attention to discern what the concerns are. One of the hard parts about being in business is that the customer is always right, even if he is wrong.
2. Be open-minded. Believe what they are telling you because they really believe they have been wronged.

250

3. Stay composed. Do not raise your voice and watch your body language so you do not communicate negatively.
4. Own the problem and make an apology for how they have felt wronged. Do not shift blame to anyone else.
5. Ask them what you can do to make this right for them.
6. Be positive focusing on things you CAN do, not what you cannot.
7. Tell them exactly how you plan to resolve the problem at hand.
8. Communicate regularly if the problem isn't resolved straight away. Thank him for his business and patience in having the issue resolved.
9. Follow up to be sure your guest is happy with the results.

Remember: Your guest is always right, even when they are wrong.

The best way to handle complaints is to head them off at the pass so you don't get them to begin with.

First, be sure your home is a good match to the customer. You don't want to put an elderly, sickly person in a remote house without a land line or cell phone coverage, stairs, soaking tubs and no shower. You don't want a person looking for a religious retreat in a party neighborhood. Listen to what your perspective guests are looking for in their travel and be candid if your house is not a good match for them.

Give written instructions on how to use items in your home. The Guest Book is the perfect place for this information.

Prepare guests for what they may encounter ahead of time. If the internet is down tell them before they arrive and give them directions to local coffee houses are with free Wi-Fi and when they can expect service to return to their property.

Lastly, keep your promises. If you tell your guests you are going to provide something-- do it. For example, if you say you have a well equipped kitchen down spices be sure there are spices in the cabinet.

Creating reasonable expectations are key here. Make sure you aren't misrepresenting your property in anyway, that guests know exactly what they are buying when they book a reservation with you.

Homework

A guest has just phoned you from your beach condominium complaining that there are no sheets and towels in the unit for them to use. It is noted in your welcome packet that you do not include these items so guest should make arrangements to bring their own. How would you handle the complaint?

_____

_____

_____

_____

_____

_____

_____

_____

_____

_____

_____

_____

_____

_____

Chapter 26
Crisis Mode

Covered in this chapter

- Real World Disasters—It Can Happen
- Consider Your Guests' Frame of Mind During a Crisis
- Distinguish Between a Major Concern and Minor Inconvenience
- Have Plans in Place to Deal with Both
- A Great Manager Avoids Problems
- Follow Up

Real World Disasters—It Can Happen

Into each life, some rain must fall. No one is exempt, no person, no government, no business, and sadly, no vacation rental. Between my experiences and Sandra's, we have dealt with a plethora of disasters, both natural and manmade, including:

Two homes hit by lightning in the same storm
Honeymooners spent winter night in their car because they couldn't get into the house
Maintenance guy passed out drunk in garage

Family of six with baby with no electricity or water

Eye of hurricane passing directly over the house—twice

Rats

Swarm of flying ants in living room

Housekeeping not having house ready after guests have flown from overseas

Roof leaking so much it made waterfall down stairs

Maid lying to guests to cover up the fact that she's having an affair

Baby opossums between the bed sheets

Tin roof leaked red colored water. Guest thought it was blood and called police

Two separate parties showed up for the same property at the same time—both with reservations

Maid stealing from guests

We could go on and on, but we might talk you out of this business! Just remember, these are the rare, once in a while events, not everyday life. Renting your home out to travelers is a great way to pay for your home and has the potential to bring in additional income, but as with any business on the planet, you have to be able to troubleshoot and deal with occasional problems. The best managers prevent problems before they start.

Consider Your Guests' Frame of Mind During a Crisis

It's hard to imagine a business in which occasional problems don't crop up. And mostly those concerns are due to unmet guest expectations. As an honest VR owner, and I know you are because you bought this book, you're going to do everything you can to make sure your guests have what they need for a lovely vacation.

Keep in mind, you can have a fabulous home but you can't prevent your guests from bringing in their own thunderstorm of problems. Sometimes, you are dealing with people who haven't had a vacation in a long time and are overwhelmed with travel, leaving their work, being with their family for 24 hours a day. All of those things create little pockets of stress for your guests. A good manager takes those things into consideration in dealing with a guest.

Distinguish Between a Major Complaint and a Minor Inconvenience

So, when you get a complaint, or *quelle heurer*, a bad review, step back and see if the problem is with your product or the guest simply failed to have a good time and are trying to get monetarily compensated. A broken air conditioning unit during the height of the summer heat is worth compensation, the amount depends on the duration. If it's fixed in an hour, it might warrant a meal out. If it is out for days, and the guests have to move or live with it, then that could be worth a partial or entire refund. However, if the temps are in the 70's, and the night air cool, then it might not be an issue. A good manager uses judgment and realizes that there are no set answers, as each problem has its own variables.

If you are fortunate, your guests have advised you of the problem while they are in your home. This is your best case scenario. You have an opportunity to immediately address their concern and possibly generating more good will toward you and your company than if they just had a moderate experience. Try to measure your reaction to the complaint. A gas leak is a very serious, potentially deadly issue, and should be dealt with urgently, starting with getting the guests out of harm's way. Ants in the kitchen are an annoyance and need to be dealt with directly, but don't require the adrenalin rush that a hazardous gas leak does.

256

Have a Plan in Place

Having information at your fingertips is helpful, both for you and your guests. Your Welcome Packet should include a page of important service number so your guests can handle minor things on their own—such as a power or cable outage. Ultimately, the responsibility is yours, so don't be annoyed or surprised when maintenance issues crop up. Simply think through those things ahead, have a plan in place, as dealing with them is part of home ownership.

When the initial call comes in, look at it from your guests' perspective. Being away from home and in new environment when an emergency or problem arises creates a lot of stress and frustration for your guests. Speak with them in a calm, authoritative way so the guests will have confidence in your ability to address their concerns in a timely manner. This will go miles towards how they feel about your home and you. If they sense undo alarm on your part, it will serve only to increase their stress levels, which is the very thing you are trying to alleviate.

A Great Manager Avoids Problems

What are some things that your area or home are prone to? If your home is on the coast, and it's prone to hurricanes, have a page in your Welcome Packet devoted to where your emergency supplies are and the evacuation route out of town. If you live in an area where wildfires are not uncommon, give your guest the emergency plan. Have a fire extinguisher and fire blanket in your kitchen. Have a water source near a fire pit. Have emergency shut off valves for water, electricity and gas clearly labeled, but do not expect your guests to deal with it. Some may have the confidence and the know-how to. Get involved in an emergency, even if you are far away.

We're spoken to how to address guests' issues and concerns in a timely manner, however, it's important to remember that some guests are just going to write a bad review.

What are some problems that could crop up in your home?

1._____

2._____

3._____

4._____

5._____

6._____

7._____

8._____

9._____

10._____

Now, write a plan for each of them. This will help put you in the mindset for solving problems when they arise.

We're going to take it a step further. Imagine you've just received a call. It could be a very sweet woman, who says, "You know, the refrigerator doesn't seem to be cooling properly." or a man who belts out, "The AC won't cool below 62 degrees. What kind of scam operation are you running here? I demand satisfaction, and right now!"

Would you treat the callers differently? If so, why?

We know what it's like to have unreasonable and demanding people barking at you, to feel backed into a corner where all you want to do is kick back at the person, but you are the manager, and your confident, pleasant, and even tone must prevail. There's a verse in Proverbs that covers this situation. "A calm answer turneth way wrath." And generally, it works.

So, I recommend the answer to both callers be, "I'm so sorry you're experiencing this problem on your vacation. I know it's frustrating. I'm going to…" then outline what you are going to do. Then, offer to phone back in a few hours to make sure the problem is fixed. See the Customer Service chapter for more details.

The key to any crisis is staying calm. Panic takes away your ability to see the lay of the land and all the possible ways to deal with it. It also takes away your objectivity. Your guests are looking to you to be the lighthouse in the storm.

If you are feeling panicky yourself and not sure of what the best route is, take a deep breath. Then say, "I'm so sorry you are dealing with this on your vacation. Thank you so much for contacting me and giving me the opportunity to correct the situation. Let me call you back in an hour (always give yourself more time than you think you'll need) and tell you how the problem will be resolved. Is that OK?"

Follow Up

Follow up is very important. If they notice one issue, there may be more. The power surge that broke your refrigerator may have also broken the toaster and the microwave, but they didn't notice it at the time.

Don't give excuses. For the vacation renter, real life is the life they lived before they came to your house, the life they lived while at your house, and the life they will go back to. At this point, they only

259

care about is the part that involves them on vacation. They are not at all interested in the fact that you just replaced that refrigerator with a brand new one and now a lightning strike has broken it. Or that your basement also flooded 6 months ago, or that the handyman that you've used for nine years is in the hospital and not only is he unavailable, but you are worried about him. That doesn't fit anywhere in their radar. What they care about is that you are a competent manager, willing to tackle this problem this day.

Homework:

Think about times when you have been away from home, and something went wrong. How was it handled?

_____
_____
_____
_____
_____
_____

How would you have handled it differently?

_____
_____
_____
_____
_____
_____

Make a policy statement for how guests are to be treated in your business.

_____
_____

Chapter 27
Reviews

Covered in this chapter

- Point Out the Negatives—if it's Three Blocks from the Beach, Say So
- Follow Up
- Make the Most of a Positive Review
- The Positive Review with a Caveat
- Dum, Dum, DUM—the Bad Review
- Constructing Your Response

It seems everyone who wants to make a purchase, whether it be a computer or dinner for two at a restaurant, checks the internet to see what other people have to say. They respect the opinion of real people much more than the carefully worded copy of the business who is selling them. While well written, compelling copy is important, but what's important to people is *"Is it true?"*

Testimonials, or good reviews, validate you as a business. They take some of the stress out of the unknown. The guests are giving you their hard earned money and taking a chance on you with their vacation time—they deserve a great vacation.

When communication the details of your property, it's important to create a picture in their head that matches reality as closely as possible. You paint a picture with words and with the photos you've chosen.

Point Out the Negatives—if it's Three Blocks from the Beach, Say So

Take a good, hard look at your VR. Take the fear out and your bias as an owner. What you say and the pictures you choose need to be truthful. Of course, a guest expects you to take pictures on sunny days, they understand that you are going to put your home in the best light, and that most places on earth, do indeed, get their share of rain.

However, are the photos misleading? Do you crop or have so many close ups that they are not giving a true picture? Be creative with your photos and words, but be honest. Read Chapters 14 and 15 for details on writing and photos for more details.

Play up a potential negative—a quick perusal of real estate ads will show you how to do this. "Starter Home" means small and simple, "As is" means has problems, but you get it at a great price. "Cute" and "quaint" often mean small. "Private" may mean a long drive from town. Be utterly truthful, if your home is three blocks from the beach, say so. Don't crowd your listing with beach photos without properly labeling them.

To get great testimonials, you have to have a great product. Make sure you stay at your VR as often as you can. For me, it's usually about every six to nine months. If it's longer than that, I hire someone in the tourism industry to do a thorough inspection. If your house is closer, make it a point to stay in it, to include each bedroom as often as is reasonable. You might be surprised at what you find. Sleep in each bed, bathe in each shower.

Build a good rapport with your guests. Phone or email them awhile after arrival, to check on things. Often, people will alert you to a problem you didn't know about, and you have a chance to fix it while they are there! You'll be the one to find out about it, not the rest of the

263

world. If they share a concern, address it immediately. Jump up and down with glee if they tell you, because you have a chance to redirect their experience. The dreaded guests are the ones who tell you everything is fine to your face, then blast you publically.

Follow Up

Once you're sure they are having a great experience, send them a quick e-mail when they get home. Here's a peek at my typical email.

Bula!

Welcome Home. I hope you had a wonderful time at Starfish Blue. We value your input, so we would love to know how your stay was. Is there anything you particularly enjoyed? Found surprising? Felt we could have done better?

Jai, Rozy, Reshmi, Mahen and I thank you for staying at Starfish Blue.

Vinaka Vakalevu,

Beth Carson

If you get a positive response, ask them to fill out a review on FlipKey or wherever you advertise online. If you get a mixed or negative response, follow up, find out what went wrong, and do whatever it takes to correct any legitimate issues immediately. Vacations are precious to people. They dream about them for months, tell all of their friends, family, and co-workers about it, and spend money and vacation time at your destination. It's someone's hopes and dreams. Treat is as the precious opportunity as it is.

Make the Most of a Positive Review

Copy and paste testimonials directly into your website—use italics, a different color, and a different font to show you're quoting someone. Sprinkle these throughout your website, instead of just having a page of testimonials.

The average review is a 4 out of 5 stars. If you reach that goal, you have met their expectations, which are generally hopefully high, but have not knocked their socks off or surprised them. This is a good job on your part and you should be pleased. Take keen note on what they didn't give you 5 stars for if it's noted.

Some people misunderstand the survey, thinking 5 stars is the equivalent of the perfect stay at the Ritz. It's not. It's meant to be how it lived up to their expectations. You wouldn't expect 1000 count sheets and high end toiletries provided at a $100/night VR. But, you would expect it to be clean and match the photos and the description and to have the appliances mentioned in the listing

The Positive Review with a Caveat

Understand that glowing testimonial after glowing testimonial can begin to sound fake. It's okay if they mention a negative. In fact, one person's negative could be another person's positive.

Our family of three stayed at a VR in Seal Beach, California. The second night, a friend from South Africa came to stay with us— this was all pre-approved with the owner.

While they advertised space for four, the place was much smaller than we expected; the walk out basement of a townhome. The bathroom was only accessible through the bedroom, and the other two beds were pull-out sofa beds in the small living room. Once the beds were opened, you had to walk on your knees across them to get from one side of the room to the other, and we had to put the luggage on the table.

265

When it was just the three of us, it was a cozy but good fit. When our friend came and we had four people, it was like being in a cage in a zoo.

I wrote a review praising the owner, the location, the décor, and mentioned that for three or fewer people, it was wonderful, but for four it was really too small. The owners husband wrote me a horrible note back, saying he wouldn't approve the review, and how could I say such things after his wife was so generous. (She truly was.)

When I asked him if he had ever tried opening both of the sofa beds, he admitted they hadn't, and thought it was a good idea to try. He was shocked to find the space was too small for it. If he had let my review go through, people would have seen a happy review with one qualifier—it honestly was too small for four, likely a fire hazard, as well.

But if you were traveling in a group of three or less, that aspect of the review wouldn't have applied to you. You would have focused on the positives I mentioned, and found the review to be helpful, because you could tell it wasn't written by the owner as a fake review.

Dum, Dum, DUM—the Bad Review

Sooner or later, you're going to get one. Maybe it was your fault, maybe it was the fact that it rained non-stop for twelve days of their vacation, and maybe they feel picked on and small and want to take their frustration out on someone they easily can—you. I'm sure you've seen reviews on many things where most people are very happy, and then you get the "Don't buy this under any circumstances—even if it's free!" Most people have a tendency to roll their eyes at those and move on. They key is having a long list of positive reviews to balance this out.

What to do if you get a bad review? First, walk away. Get some space. Vent to your spouse or friend. Complain about the unfairness of it. Tell them that you're a great owner (they already know this, of course), and just how unfair it is.

Do not make the mistake of responding immediately and portraying yourself in a manner that you would regret. And don't make the mistake that by taking a few hours or even a day to respond, that your business will be ruined.

Breathe.

Breathe again.

Now, put your manager's hat, not your owner's hat. When you're the owner, you take it personally. A manager looks at a problem and works towards a solution. They don't have the emotion that the owner has.

OK—read it again.

Take a good, hard, unemotional view of their complaints. Is this a valid complaint or a hysterical, cranky person? Pick it apart—separate the valid from the filler.

Constructing Your Response

Now, once the emotion has gone out of it as much as you can, open a Word document. Thank the person for their input. Yes, thank them. That immediately puts you in a business tone of conversation. No matter how negative and whiney and complaining the review is, rise above.

Sort out what is under your control (working appliances) and what is not (weather). Address the issues that were legit, and go ahead and mention some things in your favor—such as expressing dismay at the lack of communication while they were staying in your VR, the fact that you left contact details for just such a problem, or that you comped out a night for a non-working Jacuzzi that took a day to fix.

If the problem has been resolved, let them know. You're not talking to the guest here, as they have already formed their opinion, you're talking to your future guests and those making a decision. So watch your tone—you want to look professional, competent, and caring.

Now, don't put this out on the web just yet.

Send it to a trusted friend or family member who will tell you the truth. Send them both the review and your response. Ask them if you came across as professional, competent, and caring. Ask them if any sentences need to be taken out. No matter how hard you try, it is human nature to be defensive when attacked. You don't want to come across as defensive.

Now, sleep on it. Remember this review will likely be on the internet for years, if not forever. Don't react too quickly. Read it in the morning when you're feeling fresh, and change anything that doesn't make you sound professional, competent, and caring. Show compassion for the person who had a bad experience, sympathize with them, tell them you understand how much this vacation meant to them. Now that it's perfect, you can post your response online.

Professional Tip—as a good owner, you probably have a whole list of emails and notes you have received from happy guests. Print those out and keep them in a binder or hang them on your office wall. When you have a bad review or cranky customer, reread them. It will help!

Homework

Take a look at your listing with fresh eyes. Is there anything misleading? Rewriting any parts that aren't crystal clear.

Write a few lines in response to a positive review. The goal is to have them come back again and write a positive review online.

_____

_____

_____

_____

_____

_____

Write the opening 3 sentences to the positive review with a caveat. The goal is to highlight the positives and explain the caveat.

_____

_____

_____

_____

_____

Write an opening paragraph to a negative review. What do you start with? Remember—Thank you.

_____

_____

_____

_____

_____

_____

Some of the best money you'll ever spend. A professionally written response to a negative review.

As a writer and VR consultant, I can delve into the facts of the situation, looking at it from both sides, then craft a response that makes you sound wonderful (assuming, you are, which considering you are educating yourself by reading this book, I assume you are.)

Contact me via www.VRFusion.com to get help in your situation.

Chapter 28
Scams and Theft

Covered in this Chapter

- Signs of an E-mail Scam
- Theft
- Minimize your Risk
- What to do if Theft Occurs

Fortunately, most guests pay on time, come and have a lovely time, and leave with only their belongings. The exceptionally kind ones leave a note and a small gift as a token of their thanks. Treasure those notes. They help during the bad days.

Then, there are the very, very small percentage that you have to be on guard for. The worst is the one with the intention of harm. Most everyone who gets a decent number of inquiries will come across with one or more of these in the course of business. Trust your instincts, and if it sounds too good to be true, it probably is.

In Nigeria and other countries stricken with desperate poverty and scarce honest work, there are sweat shops where poor men try to even the scale of your abundance and their hunger. The concept has now spread to other countries, but the basis is the same. They troll listing sites for vacation rentals. Now, think logically, and you'll see right through it.

"Good day. I in the Royal Armed Forces serving in Afghanistan. I would like to give my godson a honeymoon as your condo as a wedding present. We are fine, upstanding people of our community. We wish to book your condo, and will send you a cashier's cheque immediately to secure it. I will be sending $2000 extra, if you could be so kind as to give some to our travel agent and some to my godson. We will pay you $2,000 for your extra trouble."

Huh? First, my place is a 3 bedroom house, not a condo. And I need to give money to the godson and travel agent? And $2,000 for my trouble? I don't respond to those e-mails. They are a scam. They send out thousands, and get the one who they can drag along, get an address, and send the cashier's check. They will ask for a refund, then three months from now, the bank finds out it's a scam, and you are out the money. And have damaged your credit with the bank.

Often called the Nigerian Scam, because of where many of these e-mails originate, these people prey on vacation rental owners as well as long-term rental owners. While they are getting savvier, there are red flags.

Signs of an Email Scam

Giving too much information

Not being familiar with the property (asking to rent your apartment when it's a three bedroom, two-story house)

Poor English

Very formal tone

Always paying by cashier's check or credit card, but never PayPal

Now, that's not to say that all people who use poor English or are formal are scammers, this is just a sign to look out for. If you're unsure, continue a dialogue until you know for certain one way or the other.

I had an enquiry that just didn't sound right. The name was highly unusual, and he was a single man asking for eight weeks in high season. I only had three weeks available. The e-mail was worded a little funny.

I applied my litmus test, "Will they pay using PayPal?" Generally, scammers will hop up and down, begging to get an address to send the cashier's check, but will ignore any request for payment through PayPal, they know they won't get through their stringent anti-theft policies. They always go away rather than use PayPal.

This man, however, paid immediately, a larger than needed deposit. He offered to wire or PayPal the final payment before it was due. He came, stayed for 3 weeks, left a slew of books for me on my Kindle on a USB stick as a thank you gift, joined the Starfish Blue FaceBook page, and wrote a five star review for us on TripAdvisor. I'm so glad that I didn't ignore his e-mail!

Scammers often prey on new listings, so make sure you're knowledgeable but not cynical. Always follow through with an email until you know for sure one way or the other.

Theft

While uncommon, theft is something to be aware of. Most people wouldn't dream of taking something that isn't theirs home with them. Others see nothing wrong with substituting your lovely pillows for their old ones, for taking the Glade Plug-Ins with them, for taking the towels or knickknacks.

To minimize your risk

Don't have anything of value in your home, even if it's of value to you, like your mother's figurine. Revisit the shopping chapter and look for ways to furnish your home inexpensively. If they slip out the door with something, hopefully it will be a $15 vase, and not a $300 vase.

If theft occurs

Your home is more susceptible to theft if you live in a location where people drive. Starfish Blue Fiji has never had any objects taken, but Sandra's properties in North Carolina have had theft of small items. Sandra sends them an e-mail telling them they must have accidently packed up an item in their rush to check out; it is not a problem. I will charge your credit card and send you the receipt. No one has disputed stealing something and politely getting caught. Often, it's something small, like a Glade Plug In, which she chalks up to the price of doing business.

One guest took an item (I had purchased at a flea market) and left me another in a gift bag. I didn't charge them for the item took, and happily considered it a fair trade.

If your housekeeper notices something missing, have them take a photo with their cell phone of the where the missing item should have been. As they clean, they may find it turns up in a different location, at which time they can return it to its regular spot, then delete the photo. If it turns out to be truly missing, send your guest a bill.

Typically, guests will be overly cautious in making sure they do not take advantage of your VR. You might receive a phone call or email for minimal damage done by a guest like a broken glass or bleached out towel. Those are considered standard wear and tear, not theft or damage.

Sandra finds that the item most often missing is hair dryers. She doesn't believe it is an intentional theft, simply an error in packing up the bathroom (imagine asking a husband to pack the bathroom—he would assume the dryer belonged to his wife). She is moving towards wall mounted dryers as the standard dryers disappear.

I have had extraordinary luck with guests being honest with broken items. All the guests have admitted it, pointed it out to the maids or manager, and offered to pay. I have never allowed them to pay, as a broken coffee pot, refrigerator handle, or rice cooker is the price of doing business. And it leaves the guest with a good feeling that they are being looked after in a quality home.

Final Thoughts

Congratulations on educating yourself on the vacation rental market. Look at what you've learned!

The last few chapters could have scared you off, but I hope they didn't. The book wouldn't have been complete without some warnings, but knowledge it power. Thankfully, Cranky Customers, the Bad Review, Crisis Mode, and Theft and Scams are the exception, not the rule.

If you feel overwhelmed by the possible downside, please keep in mind that both Sandra and I have laid all of our trials and traumas open for you to learn from, especially in the last few chapters. These hard bits of earned wisdom come over a period of 9 years- a combined 18 years' experience in this business. The majority of days are fun and uneventful.

Of course, a book based on happy days would be fun but lacking in substance. But don't make the mistake of thinking this is a routine part of business. These are the exceptions.

Our days often involve happy encounters with future and past guests and some days involve depositing money into bank accounts- for Sandra, that's a daily occurrence with 16 properties. You'll get to talk with people planning a vacation. It's a fun job. After your guests have a great experience, you'll get notes when they come back saying what a lovely time. We love this business!

The hard parts are those rare days in between. If you follow the advice within this cover and purchase a sound home that is well suited for a vacation rental and run your business as a professional, putting yourself in your guests' place and making decisions that are beneficial to them, you have a very good chance of becoming a huge success. Or at least meeting reasonable goals- like offsetting costs.

Of course, there are no guarantees, but you already know that.

Let me be the first to welcome you to your second home and new business.

Beth

Join the conversation at www.VRFusion.com

You don't have to go it alone!

If you feel overwhelmed and need a coach or consultant, Beth is available to provide personal assistance with your particular situation. Group coaching options are available for low cost, ongoing help. Both Sandra and Beth are available for half and full day training at property management companies.

To Your Success!

Made in the USA
Lexington, KY
21 March 2014